FEDERAL FINANCE

FEDERAL FINANCE

An Alternative Basis for Allocation of Resources

O.P. CHOPRA

CONCEPT PUBLISHING COMPANY, NEW DELHI

First Published 1985

Om Prakash Chopra (*b.* 1941-)

Published by
Naurang Rai
Concept Publishing Company
H-13, Bali Nagar
NEW DELHI-110015 (India)

Printed in India by
Ajit Singh
Printco India
Maujpur, Delhi-110053

PREFACE

THIS study originated in an academic curiosity to find out an alternative basis to the allocation of resources. Are the States justified in their criticism that the allocation of resources from the Centre to States has been inadequate? Is it true that some States have been discriminated against as reflected in the allocation of resources to them?

A lot of academic debt has accumulated during the course of this study. I am extremely grateful to Prof. A.B. Ghosh for his invaluable guidance during the initial period of study. Thanks are due to Prof. A.M. Khusro and Prof. B.V. Krishnamurthy who helped me with their incisive comments and suggestions. I had the benefit of discussing some of the issues raised in this study with Prof. U.K. Hicks. It was really generous on her part to have spared time and offer valuable comments. Dr. Kanchan Chopra had been instrumental in bringing to my notice certain weaknesses in the arguments and went through the entire manuscript.

I am grateful to the editors of the Indian Economic Review, the Indian Economic Journal and the Review of Commerce Studies for allowing me to include a modified version of my papers in these journals.

The work would not have completed but for the continued support I received from Prof. M.M. Anand, the Dean, Faculty of Management Studies, University of Delhi; Prof. Abad Ahmad, Director South Campus, University of Delhi and my colleagues at the Faculty of Management Studies.

O.P. CHOPRA

CONTENTS

LIST OF TABLES

1

FEDERAL FINANCE

An Alternative Approach to Allocation of Resources

FINANCIAL relations between the Union Government and the State Governments in India have remained an unsettled problem, a solution of which has assumed an added significance on account of the emergence of non-Congress Governments in a number of States since 1968. Even when the Congress party ruled at the Centre as well as in all the States some of the latter were very critical of the decision of the Union Government about transfer of resources. The search for a rational approach uniformly applied to all the States has continued.

In this study we suggest an approach for allocation of resources from the Union Government to the States. This approach is primarily guided by consideration of equity and is beneficial to economically less developed States. Possible growth retarding effect of the recommendations has been taken care of by relevant modifications to the approach to protect the interests of the economically advanced States. The results incorporating these modifications have also been worked out and are given in Chapter 5.

It is true that in determining the quantum of resources to be given to each State, it is the total transfer that should be considered. Transfers both on capital as well as current account have an impact on the financial position of a State. We have decided to restrict our study to the transfer of resources on current account on several considerations. First, computation of optimum transfer of resources on capital account involves the difficulty of measurement of marginal efficiency of capital. Second, factors other than economic affect decisions relating to this category of transfers. Again, it is the difficulty in identifying the influence of political factors and other factors which dissuaded us from incorporating the effect of other than economic factors. Finally, determination of the magnitude of desired transfer on current account is itself a heavy task; and if with this is combined that of computing desired allocation on capital account, it may become considerably difficult task. We are aware of the limited value of a study on current account. But this exercise has its relevance in as much as the objective of allocation on capital account may be different. For example, it may be guided by rapid rate of growth and the allocation pattern follows a pattern such that the returns are the highest. Alternatively, the objective may be balanced regional growth, or maximisation of generation of employment or removal of poverty. Therefore, the results arrived at in this study can be treated as a set of first stage results. These can be taken into account in arriving at the magnitude of total transfers provided there is no conflict in the objectives that are envisaged to be achieved through the allocation of resources on current account and capital account. Allocation of resources on capital account and the interdependence of expenditure on capital account and current account can be a subject of a separate study.

This study is based on a number of simplifying assumptions. First, expenditure incurred by one State is independent of that incurred by other States. This may be true to a limited extent. In fact, whenever there is a revision in the pay-scales of the Central Government employees it has a snow-balling effect. Recall that the Seventh Finance Commission was specifically assigned the task of incorporating the effect of expected rise in the pay-scales of Government employees in making its recommendations on transfer of resources. But, the expenditure on other heads such as education, medical health, irrigation, public works may not be influenced significantly by that incurred by other States.

Second, the resources available with the Union Government are large enough to meet the requirements of all the States. Recall that one of the terms of reference of the Seventh Finance Commission was to keep in view the resources available with the Central Government. The other Commissions too, must have been guided by the availability of resources of the Central Government. But, the President of India, in its authority to constitute the Commission, must have been guided by special reasons in framing availability of resources as one of the specific terms of reference. In the computations this assumption has been given up by us in arriving at the final set of results.

Third, there is a unilateral flow of resources from the Union Government to the States. This implies that if the desired transfer to a State is less than zero, it is not required to repay this amount to the Union. It is obvious that it is difficult to expect a State to repay some money to the Union Government because the resources of the State Governments are somewhat inelastic.

From the arguments given above, it follows that the proposed approach does not conform to the provisions laid down under the Constitution. This is explicable because we are presenting an alternative approach to the allocation of resources. These results of desired transfer can be compared with the actual transfers under the recommendations of different Finance Commissions. Note that the desired transfer worked out by us seeks to remove some of the contradictions in the basis on which the allocation of resources depends. For example, the allocation of revenue from income tax is to be guided by (a) population and (b) collection. Similarly, the basis of allocation of Union excise duties is (a) population, (b) per capita income, (c) number of persons below the poverty line and so on. For details see Appendix IV. We may mention that Prof. Raj Krishna in his Minute of Dissent has suggested a formula for allocation of resources. According to this formula a State is entitled to resources out of the common pool in the ratio of the product of two factors: (i) inverse of per capita income and (ii) number of persons below the poverty line. The difference caused to resources to different States is given in Appendix V.

The overview of the study is as follows : In Chapter 2, we survey the studies on different theoretical approaches to the problem of allocation of resources. These fall into three groups, viz. (i) efficiency oriented approaches, (ii) equity approaches and (iii) a combination of these two approaches. Chapter 3 discusses some simple models analysing the impact of different types of changes (viz. equal absolute change, equal proportionate change, inequal proportionate change) in expenditure and revenue on the comparative grant received by a State. In Chapter 4 we present the methodology of our study. Chapter 5 analyses the results relating to different States under different sets of assumptions. Chapter 6 presents an analysis of justness of actual transfers. The basis of comparison is provided by the formula (i) given by Nixon Administration, (ii) Advisory Commission on Inter-Governmental Relations, (iii) recommended in this study, and (iv) actual transfers as per the recommendations of different Finance Commissions. Chapter 7 presents a summary of findings and indicates fields of further exploration.

2

ALLOCATION OF RESOURCES AMONG STATES IN A FEDERATION

A Survey of Theoretical Approaches

VARIOUS approaches have been suggested as the basis for the allocation of fiscal resources between the constituent units of a federation. These can be divided into three broad categories. The first category, which we shall call 'efficiency oriented approach' advanced by Scott and others[1] will be examined in Section I. The second based primarily on considerations o 'equity in fiscal pressures' formulated by James Buchanan[2] will be considered in Section II. The third based on equity, subject however to the tax effort of each State, will be considered in Section III. Richard A. Musgrave's approach[3] (particularly his plans IV, V and VI) falls in this category. Section IV critically examines the studies relating primarily to India. The final section gives a brief outline of the approach to be pursued in this study.

SECTION I

Scott's approach[4] to the allocation of resources is based solely on considerations of efficiency. The most efficient allocation is defined as that in which non-labour resources are combined with labour in such a manner that the marginal productivity of similar units of labour is the same in all the States. This requires labour to be perfectly mobile as between the States. Any transfer of non-labour resources from the *rich* to the *poor*

States[5] through Central grants will be resource distorting as it will reduce labour mobility and prevent equalization of marginal productivity. This is elucidated by Scott in his second paper.[6] Transfer of resources to poor States results in a higher level of social amenities. So, if labour in a poor State takes into account the level of wages as well as that of social services his incentive to migrate to a richer State will be reduced by the given transfer of resources. To the argument that the consequential higher level of social services in the poor State could mean a more efficient labour force which will attract additional non-labour resources from other States, Scott replies that poor States being by definition less favourably endowed with natural resources will yield a lower dividend on the non-labour resources than the rich States leading to a less than optimal situation.

SECTION II

Buchanan's[7] approach is based primarily on considerations of 'equity in fiscal pressure' which represents the difference between taxes paid and benefits derived from public services. He emphasises that fiscal pressure rather than taxation alone is the appropriate criterion of equity, for individuals with equal income (hereafter called equals) become subjected to unequal fiscal pressure if taxation is the same but the level and/or range of services supplied varies. He points out that in a federation different political units (like Federal Government, State Government and Local Bodies) have autonomy in levying taxes and providing services. Each of these economically heterogeneous units may treat equals at par in taxation but this will not ensure same fiscal pressure for equals living in different States because the level of public services in States with lower fiscal capacity (lower per capita income) will tend to be lower compared to rich States. On equity considerations this is not justified and hence resources should be transferred from rich to poor States to achieve equality in fiscal pressures. Further, he argues that higher fiscal pressure in poor States compared to that in rich States will provide an incentive to resources to migrate to rich

States thereby preventing the free market mechanism from determining optimal allocation of resources. The desirability of minimising this strengthens the case for transfer of resources from rich to poor States.[8]

As seen above Buchanan holds that efficiency need not be the sole criterion in determining the pattern of allocation of resources as priority may be attached to equity including removal of regional disparities. Even when it is,[9] a transfer of resources from the rich to the poor States[10] is not always resource distorting. This is proved as follows : there are three different kinds of transfer, viz. (i) differential income taxation as between States, (ii) unconditional equalizing[11] grants and (iii) conditional equalizing grants. The first will be resource distorting only if all human resource units are homogeneous in the sense that sensitivity with respect to taxation is the same, for, then alone it will reduce mobility. As the assumption of labour homogeneity is not correct in real life the effect of differential income taxation cannot be generalised as adverse. The argument establishing resource distortion also assumes other resources to be geographically immobile which is not true.

The impact of the second kind of transfer would vary with the reaction of the State Governments. Possible reactions are e.g. (i) a reduction in taxes with the same level of services and (ii) an improvement in the level of services.[12] No clearly discernible pattern of resource distortion or 'correction' through labour movement emerges in the first case. A reduction in the property tax, for instance, will not have any resource effect in the short run; in the long run, however, it may, via a reduction of rents. If the reduction is in an indirect tax say, excise duties, the "hidden nature" of tax may prevent any noticeable effect.[13] Impact of an improvement or expansion in public services would vary according to the kind of service. For example, improved highways may have very little effect on the mobility of human resources.[14] Improvement of education may increase the ratio of skilled to unskilled labour, thereby attracting additional non-labour resources.

The effect of the third kind of transfer will depend upon the kind of public service to which it relates and the impact will be similar to that pointed out above.[15]

Scott[16] has demonstrated the compatibility of diametrically opposite solutions to the allocation of resources provided by him and Buchanan. He mentions "We seem agreed that demand is based on marginal productivity of each kind of labour. My point was that the poor the area (in my sense poor in natural resources) the lower the demand curve will be and lower the rewards will tend to be. Buchanan's point was that (for any fixed endowments of natural advantage) the more the capital can be induced to immigrate the higher the demand curve will be. The two points are formally compatible and it can be concluded that mobile factors should shift to where demand is highest. Buchanan concludes that demand should be raised where resources are fixed." Thus Scott considers the difference in the definition of poor State as the explanation for different solutions.[17]

SECTION III

The third approach to the problem of allocation of resources is based on consideration of equity, subject however to the tax effort of each State. This is emphasized in a number of recent contributions specially with reference to the United States.[18] The most lucid theoretical exposition of this stand is to be found in Musgrave's study.[19] It may be noted that in these contributions tax effort of a State seems to have replaced 'marginal productivity' of resources invested in it as a criterion of efficiency. Musgrave considers a number of plans with different objectives and their impact on State tax revenue.[20]

The objective of fourth, fifth and sixth plans is to bring about equality corrected by some weight for a State's own tax effort. Hence these plans are a combination of efficiency approach[21] and equity approach. The first (Musgrave's IVth) plan in this group seeks to equalize fiscal capacity. Each State is entitled to a subsidy equal to the difference between the revenue which would be obtained if its tax rate was applied to the average tax base (total tax base of the federation divided by the number of units) and the revenue which is obtained by applying its tax rate to its own base. The scheme of grants has to clear[22] the central budget. This plan will result in a redistribution from States with large tax bases to States with smaller bases. If tax rates in States with large tax base are high relative to those with small tax base the gainers will include some States with above average tax base. Further, States with a tax base below the average will be better off/ worse off if their own tax rate is high/low as compared to the average rate.

The objective of the second (Musgrave's Vth) plan in this group is to enable States to achieve the same performance level per dollar of their own tax effort. A State is entitled to a subsidy equal to the difference between its index of needs and the average need index (i.e. for the entire country) multiplied by self-financed (tax) outlay. This amount is to be adjusted to clear the central budget. There will be a redistribution from less needy to more needy States. If tax yields are high in high need States, the gaining group will include States with more than average need. If yields are relatively high in low need States, the gaining group will include some States with less than average need. Further, States with more/less than average need will be better off/worse off if their tax rate is high/low as compared to the average tax.

The objective of the third plan (Musgrave's VIth) is to equalize difference between fiscal capacity and need taking into account State's own efforts as measured by its tax rate. This plan is thus an amalgam of the previous two plans. A State is entitled to a subsidy representing sum of two parts adjusted to clear the central budget. The first part measures the difference in tax revenue obtained by applying the tax rate of the given State to the average tax base as compared to what is obtained by applying its tax rate to its own tax base. The second part represents the difference in the index of need of the given State and the average need multiplied by the tax that will be raised by applying its tax rate to the average of tax base. This plan will result in a redistribution from low-need-large-base States to high-need-small-base States. The States with high-need-small-base are better off if their tax rates are high while the States with low-need-small-base will be better off if their tax rates are low.

We might mention here that objective of the seventh plan of Musgrave is to give incentive by a system of matching grants where the central fisc matches all State revenues or outlays at a uniform rate. This plan which is purely efficiency oriented, results in opposite redistributive effects to those of earlier plans. It can be concluded that Musgrave's analysis gives content to a number of issues implicit in approaches of equity and efficiency. The assumptions are stated clearly[23] and a set of generalisations is arrived at. From the point of view of this section plans fourth, fifth and sixth are relevant. Hence, we have considered these plans with their redistributive effects in detail.

SECTION IV

In this section, we shall focus our attention on the studies that deal with the problem in the context of underdeveloped countries, more particularly India. A number of politically oriented studies have been made.[24] Then there are studies that comment on the procedure actually adopted for determining allocation.[25] Further there are studies that compare India with other Federations like U.S.A., Australia and Canada.[26] All these aspects of Centre-State financial relations do not fall within our purview. We shall restrict our survey to studies that provide an economic basis for the allocation of resources between States in the light of the three categories given earlier.

A study that recommends a purely efficiency based approach is by Tripathi.[27] He argues that in an underdeveloped economy the objective of attaining the maximum rate of growth is primary and welfare considerations that suggest equitable distribution of fruits of development are secondary.[28] On the ground of economic efficiency his stand is unquestionable. But the economic plans of most underdeveloped nations work within the limitations of political workability, which provides a limit to the extent to which resources can be allocated strictly on the basis of efficiency oriented approach. This is the stand taken by the studies we consider below.

Lakdawala's approach[29] for instance, amounts to a combination of the two approaches (efficiency approach and the equity approach). Grants from the Centre to the States, he argues, should be classified into equalisation grants and developmental grants. The former are to be used to ensure that a State exploiting its resources properly, does not fall behind the All-India average. In other words, they are to be used to ensure a certain degree of balance in regional growth. The developmental grants, on the other hand, should be used to maximize growth within a given time horizon.

Sastri[30] also recommends that after determining the magnitude of desired transfer on the basis of needs (which is purely equity approach) we should modify these results by a correcting factor. This factor measures the tax effort made and economy affected in incurring expenditure (by reducing avoidable expenditure) by a State. To measure the tax effort made, he suggests a procedure to compute tax raising capacity (as given in our chapter on methodology). He recommends that the difference between the actual revenue obtained through State taxation and computed tax raising capacity provides a measure of maladjustment. The amount representing maladjustment is to be added or deducted from the desired transfer to yield corrected desired allocation.[31] Zaveri's approach[32] has some similarities with Sastri's approach.

Government of India[33] has also accepted a criteria for allocation of central assistance for the Fourth Plan period which lays great emphasis on equity. According to this scheme, sixty per cent of the total allocation is to be made on the basis of population and ten per cent on their per capita income if below the national average; both of these are equity criteria.

SECTION V

The approach adopted by us starts with an extreme case of equity where standard expenditure on all the heads is calculated on the basis of population. Gradual modification gives credit to economically advanced States. In the next stage, standard expenditure on different heads is calculated on the basis of selected appropriate characteristics. Further, the computation of standard tax revenue without attaching any weightage to per capita income of a State and on proportionate basis (as described in the chapter of methodology) results in increasing the magnitude of desired transfer to the economically advanced States. Finally, the results of desired transfer as calculated in the preceding stage are multiplied by a certain weight representing efficiency defined on the guidelines of Musgrave. These results further increase the magnitude of desired transfer to economically advanced States.

Notes and References

1 See A.D., Scott, A note on grants in federal countries, *Economica*, New Series, Vol. XVII (November 1950), pp. 416-22; and Tripathi, R.N., *Federal Finance in a Developing Economy*, Calcutta, World Press, 1961.

2 J.M. Buchanan, Federalism and fiscal equity, *American Economic Review*, Vol. XL (September 1950), pp. 582-99.

3 R.A. Musgrave, Approaches to a fiscal theory of political federalism, in NBER, *Public Finances: Needs, Sources and Utilisation*, edited James Buchanan, Princeton University Press, 1961, pp. 97-122.

4 A.D. Scott, *op. cit.*, f.n. 1.

5 According to Scott, a rich State is endowed with relatively better natural resources.

6 A.D. Scott, Federal grants and resource allocation, *Journal of Political Economy*, No. 6, Vol. LX (1952), pp. 534-38.

7 J.M. Buchanan, *op. cit.*, f.n. 2.

8 I may point out that advocates of 'efficiency approach' may say that the incentive to migrate from poor to rich States expedited by fiscal pressures is a step in the right direction.

9 J.M. Buchanan, Federal grants and resource allocation, *Journal of Political Economy*, No. 3, Vol. LX (1952), pp. 208-14.

10 According to him, the handicap of a poor State in natural resources (as defined by Scott) can be reduced.

11 Equalizing means that more money is transferred per capita to low income States. This paper of Buchanan when read with his earlier paper will interpret equalizing grants as those which equalize 'fiscal pressure' between States.

12 The normal situation would probably be some combination of tax reduction and expenditure expansion.

13 His argument may be supplemented. The impact of an excise duty depends on a number of variables e.g., the proportion of tax to the total cost per unit of output, the nature of demand for the product, the proportion of the total consumption expenditure to the expenditure on the item and so on.

14 Except between adjacent areas where also it will be marginal.

15 For the impact of conditional and unconditional grants on the achievement of higher social indifference curve, see A.D. Scott, Evaluation of federal grants, *Economica*, New Series, Vol. XIX (Nov. 1952), pp. 374-94; and Thurow, Lester, The theory of grants-in-aid, *National Tax Journal*, Vol. XIX (December 1966), pp. 373-77.

16 A.D. Scott, *op. cit.*, f.n. 6.

17 We may record here the observation of J.R. Hicks, The nature and basis of economic growth, in U.K. Hicks (Ed.), *Federalism and Economic Growth in Underdeveloped Areas*, London, Allen and Unwin, 1961, pp. 70-80, on this controversy which is that the debate relates to development rather than efficiency; equalizing grants impose growth-slowing tax-burden on richer States which has been interpreted differently by Scott and Buchanan; also both authors have not taken account of the presence of unemployment in rich or poor States. Also see A.D. Scott, Economic goals of federal finance, *Public Finance*, No. 3, Vol. XIX (1964), pp. 241-88, for further elucidation of his preference for efficiency approach.

18 Thomas D. Hopkins, Income distribution in grants-in-aid equity analysis, *National Tax Journal*, Vol. XVIII (1965), pp. 209-13. He suggests that a State's median income can be taken as an index of both its need and fiscal capacity, former reflecting the equity approach and the latter the efficiency approach.

19 R.A. Musgrave, *op. cit.*, f.n. 3.

20 The objective of the first three plans is establishment of equity irrespective of the tax effort of the State, seeking to equalize per capita State outlay, performance levels of public services taking into account the index of need and difference between need and fiscal capacity respectively.

21 Efficiency as defined by Musgrave pointed out earlier.

22 This is on account of the assumption that sum of subsidies is equal to zero.

23 For assumptions and their limitations see Musgrave, *op. cit.*, f.n. 3. For separate treatment of spill-over effects which is one of the assumptions of Musgrave's approach, see C.M. Tiebout, An economic theory of fiscal decentralization, in NBER, *op. cit.*, f.n. 3, pp. 79-96. Also refer G.A. Akerlof, Centre-state fiscal relations in India, *Indian Economic Review*, Vol. IV (October 1969), pp. 1-12; N.A. Haskell, Federal grants-in-aid, their influence on state and local expenditure, *Canadian Journal of Economics and Political*

Science, No. 4, Vol. XXX (November 1964), pp. 585-91; and J.W. Osman, Dual impact of federal aid on state and local government expenditure, *National Tax Journal*, Vol. XIX (1966), pp. 362-72, for the impact of spill-over effects of the public services on the welfare of the country and the effect of grants on the performance level of the public services in the State concerned respectively.

24 Asok Chanda, *Federalism in India, a Study of Union-State Relations*, London, Allen and Unwin, 1965; R.N. Bhargava, (The) *Theory and Working of Union Finance in India*, London, Allen and Unwin, 1956; and B.P. Adarkar, *Principles and Problems on Federal Finance*, London P.S. King, 1933.

25 K. Santhanam, Financial relations between the union and the states, *Commerce* (Annual), Vol. 111, No. 2852 (December 1965), pp. 34-36 and his other papers.

26 B.N. Ganguli, Federal-state financial relations in U.S.A., Canada and Australia and their lessons for India, in *Changing India—Essays in honour of D.R. Gadgil*, 1961; and U.K. Hicks, Current problems of federal finances in India and some comparisons with Australia, *Public Finance*, No. 3, Vol. XXIII (1968), pp. 221-45.

27 R.N. Tripathi, *op. cit.*, f.n. 1, pp. 1-2.

28 He goes on to argue how efficiency criteria when applied to a federation comprising of constituent States may lead to a different optimum from that where a federation does not exist. We shall not go into these details. See Tripathi, *ibid*.

29 D.T. Lakdawala, Some problems of Indian federal finance, *Commerce* (Annual), Vol. 111, No. 2852 (December 1965), pp. 38-43. Also see D.T. Lakdawala, *Union-State Financial Relations*, Bombay, Lalvani Publishing House, 1967.

30 K.V.S. Sastri, *Federal-State Fiscal Relations in India*, London, Oxford University Press, 1966.

31 It may be noted that while actually computing the amount of desired transfer he does not adjust the amount of desired transfer for either tax effort or economy affected in incurring expenditure. He simply works out the results of desired transfers on three different assumptions. According to the first assumption, the desired transfer is to be computed on the basis of an index representing inverse of the per capita income of the given State. The second assumption computes desired transfer on the basis of population. Under the third, desired allocation to a State is determined 90% on the basis of the capita income and 10% on the basis of the area of the State.

32 N.J. Zaveri, Transfer of non-plan resources to states, *Economic and Political Weekly*, Vol. IV, No. 23 (June 7, 1969), pp. 939-43. According to his approach 70% of the total divisible pool may be divided on the basis of population. This may be adjusted if there are

special problems like density of population, scheduled tribes population and so on. To encourage States to mobilize resources 10% of the transfer may be distributed on the basis of taxation by the States in relation to their State's income. Another 10% of the resources may be transferred to those States whose per capita income is below the average. The remaining 10 per cent may be distributed to those States whose per capita developmental expenditure is below the National average.

33 Government of India, Administrative Reforms Commission, *Report on Centre-State Relationships*, June 1969, p. 11.

3

SOME SIMPLE MODELS FOR ALLOCATION OF RESOURCES

THE basic approach adopted in our study suggests that the grant received by a State should be equal to the difference between standard expenditure and standard revenue.[1]

Thus

$G_i = E_i - R_i$, where G_i is grant received by State i

E_i is standard expenditure of State i

and R_i is standard revenue of State i.

In this chapter, we shall discuss various models for analysing the impact of changes in E_i and R_i.

Changes in the expenditure and revenue of a State are divided into three types. In Model I, we analyse the impact of an equal absolute change, first in expenditure and then in revenue. Model II considers how an equal proportionate change in the expenditure or the revenue of the different States affects the comparative magnitude of grants received by them. Model III analyses the effect of an unequal proportionate change in either expenditure or revenue raising capacity. Models IV and V study the impact of simultaneous changes in expenditure and revenue taking respectively an equal proportionate change and an unequal proportionate change as between the different States. It may be noted that, we shall primarily be interested in the magnitude of the grant received by a State relative to the average of the grant received by all the States. We are thus looking at the position of a State, relative to other States, before and after the change. As the primary purpose here shall be to consider extremely simplified situations, and to bring to focus the basic issues involved, we shall retain throughout, the following simplifying assumptions : (*a*) changes in the expenditure and revenue of a State are independent of those of other States; (*b*) resources of the Centre are perfectly elastic so that they respond readily to changes in the magnitude of grants; (*c*) movement of funds is always unilateral so that grants flow only from the Centre to the States, so that $G_i > 0$[2] or $G \not< 0$, and (*d*) expenditure and revenue are looked at from macro angle, the components of these not being taken into account.

Model I :

For any State '*i*' $G_i = E_i - R_i$[3] ...(1.1)

Let K represent an absolute increase in expenditure of State '*i*'[4]. Revenue is assumed to remain constant, so that

$$E_i' = E_i + K \text{ and } R'_i = R_i$$

$$G'_i = E_i' - R'_i = E_i + K - R_i \qquad \text{...(1.2)}$$

Define $$\bar{G} = \frac{\sum_{i=1}^{n} G_i}{n} = \frac{E_c - R_c}{n}\text{[5]}$$

where E_c = sum of E_i's for all States

$$= \sum_{i=1}^{n} E_i$$

and $$R_c = \sum_{i=1}^{n} R_i$$

Then $$\bar{G}' = \sum_{i=1}^{n} \frac{G'_i}{n} = \frac{E'_c - R'_c}{n} = \frac{\Sigma(E_i + K) - \Sigma R_i}{n}$$

$$=\frac{\sum_{i=1}^{n} E_i+Kn-\sum_{i=1}^{n} R_i}{n}=\frac{E_c-R_c+nK}{n}$$

The change in the grant received by a State relative to the average grant is given by

$$G'_i/\bar{G}'-G_i/\bar{G}=\frac{E_i+K-R_i}{\frac{E_c-R_c+nK}{n}}-\frac{E_i-R_i}{\frac{E_c-R_c}{n}}$$

$$=\frac{nK[(E_c-R_c)-n(E_i-R_i)]^{6}}{(E_c-R_c)\ (E_c-R_c+nK)} \quad ...(1.3)$$

Now, $G'_i/\bar{G}'\gtrless G_i/\bar{G}$ if $\bar{G}\gtrless G_i$ ...(1.4)

From condition (1.4) it follows that States receiving a grant less than/more than the average before the change stand to gain/lose by an absolute increase in expenditure, the position of the average State remaining unchanged. The impact of an absolute decrease in expenditure (which is the same as that of an absolute increase in revenue) on the comparative grant received by a State will be just the opposite.

Initially $\quad G_i=E_i-R_i$ ...(1)

An absolute increase in the revenue raising capacity of every State takes place, expenditure remaining the same.

Such that $\quad R'_i=R_i+K$ and $E'_i=E_i$.

$$G'_i=E'_i-R'_i=E_i-(R_i+K)=E_i-R_i-K \quad ...(2)$$

As before $\quad \bar{G}=\sum_{i=1}^{n}\frac{G_i}{n}=\frac{E_c-R_c}{n}$

However, now $\quad \bar{G}'=\sum_{i=1}^{n}\frac{G'_i}{n}=\frac{\Sigma(E'_i-R'_i)}{n}$

$$=\frac{\Sigma E_i-\Sigma R_i-nK}{n}=\frac{E_c-R_c-nK}{n}$$

$$G'_i/\bar{G}'-G_i/\bar{G}=\frac{n(E_i-R_i-K)}{E_c-R_c-nK}-\frac{n(E_i-R_i)}{E_c-R_c}$$

or $\quad G'_i/\bar{G}'-G_i/\bar{G}=nK\frac{[n(E_i-R_i)-(E_c-R_c)]}{(E_c-R_c)\ (E_c-R_c-nK)}$ ...(3)

Therefore $G'_i/\bar{G}' \gtrless G_i/\bar{G}$ if $\bar{G}_i \gtrless \bar{G}$ ...(4)

From condition (4) it follows that States with an initial grant greater/less than the average gain/lose by an absolute increase in revenue, the position of the average State remaining unchanged.

Model II :

This model analyses the effect of an equal proportionate increase in expenditure of different States on the comparative grants received by them.

Initially $G_i = E_i - R_i$ ...(2.1)

Let the expenditure of every State increase by a proportion 'p'

Then $E'_i = E_i(1+p)$

$R_i' = R_i$

Hence $G'_i = E'_i - R'_i = E_i(1+p) - R_i$ ...(2.2)

As before, $$\bar{G} = \sum_{i=1}^{n} \frac{G_i}{n} = \frac{\Sigma(E_i - R_i)}{n} = \bar{E} - \bar{R}$$

where $$\bar{E} = \sum_{i=1}^{n} \frac{E_i}{n} \text{ and } \bar{R} = \sum_{i=1}^{n} \frac{R_i}{n}$$

But $$\bar{G}' = \sum_{i=1}^{n} \frac{G'_i}{n} = \sum_{i=1}^{n} [E(1+p) - R_i] = (1+p)\bar{E} - \bar{R}$$

$$\frac{G'_i}{\bar{G}'} - \frac{G_i}{\bar{G}} = \frac{E_i(1+p) - R_i}{\bar{E}(1+p) - \bar{R}} - \frac{E_i - R_i}{\bar{E} - \bar{R}}$$

After simplifying $$\frac{G'_i}{\bar{G}'} - \frac{G_i}{\bar{G}} = \frac{p(\bar{E}R_i - E_i\bar{R})}{[\bar{E}(1+p) - \bar{R}][\bar{E} - \bar{R}]} \quad ...(2.3)$$

From (2.3) it follows that

$G'_i/\bar{G}' \gtrless G_i/\bar{G}$ if $\bar{E}/\bar{R} \gtrless E_i/R_i$ ...(2.4)

From condition (2.4) it is clear that in the case of an equal proportionate increase in expenditure, the ratio of a State's expenditure to its revenue compared to average of this ratio determines whether it is relatively a gainer, loser or unaffected by the change. For States with a ratio of expenditure to revenue less /more than the average, the change means a gain/loss, the position of the States with a ratio equal to the average remaining unaffected. The impact of an equal proportionate decrease in expenditure (which is the same as that of an equal proportionate increase in revenue) on the comparative grants received by them will be the opposite of that mentioned above. As postulated earlier $G_i = E_i - R_i$...(1). In this case, revenue raising capacity of a State increases by a proportion 'q' and expenditure remains constant so that

$$R'_i = R_i(1+q)$$

$$\text{and } E'_i = E_i$$

Therefore $$G'_i = E'_i - R'_i = E_i - R_i(1+q) = E_i - R_i - R_i q \qquad \text{...(2)}$$

As before $$\bar{G} = \sum_{i=1}^{n} \frac{G_i}{n} = \frac{\Sigma(E_i - R_i)}{n} = \frac{\Sigma E_i}{n} - \frac{\Sigma R_i}{n}$$

$$= \bar{E} - \bar{R}$$

$$\text{and } \bar{G}' = \sum_{i=1}^{n} \frac{G'_i}{n} = \frac{\Sigma[E_i - R_i(1+q)]}{n}$$

$$= \frac{\Sigma E_i}{n} - \frac{(1+q)\Sigma R_i}{n}$$

$$= \bar{E} - (1+q)\bar{R}$$

$$G'_i/\bar{G}' - G_i/\bar{G} = \frac{E_i - R_i(1+q)}{\bar{E} - \bar{R}(1+q)} - \frac{E_i - R_i}{\bar{E} - \bar{R}}$$

$$= \frac{q(E_i\bar{R}_i - R_i\bar{E})}{[(\bar{E} - \bar{R})][(\bar{E} - \bar{R}(1+q))]} \qquad \text{...(3)}$$

From (3), it follows that

$$G'_i/\bar{G}' \gtrless G_i/\bar{G} \text{ if } E_i/R_i \gtrless \bar{E}/\bar{R} \qquad \text{...(4)}$$

From (4) it follows that an equal proportionate increase in revenue results in a comparative gain/loss for States having a ratio of expenditure to revenue greater/less than the average, the position of the State with a ratio equal to the average remains unaffected.

It may be noted that the basic difference between Model I and Model II (an absolute change and a proportionate change in expenditure or revenues) relates to the fact that in Model I the relationship between grant to the given State to the average grant determines its comparative positions while in Model II the relationship between the ratio of expenditure to the revenue of the given State to that of the average ratio determines comparative allocation from the Centre.

Model III :

In this model we consider the impact of an unequal proportionate increase in expenditure of different States on the comparative grants received by them with an unchanged revenue.

As before $G_i = E_i - R_i$ ...(3.1)

Now expenditure of State 'i' increases by a proportion p_i.[7]

So that $E'_i = E_i(1+p_i)$ and $R'_i = R_i$

Hence $G'_i = E'_i - R'_i = E_i(1+p_i) - R_i$

$$= E_i + x_i - R_i \qquad ...(3.2)$$

where $x_i = p_i . E_i$

$$\bar{G} = \sum_{i=1}^{n} \frac{G_i}{n} = \frac{\sum_{i=1}^{n} (E_i - R_i)}{n} = \bar{E} - \bar{R}$$

$$\text{and } \bar{G}' = \sum_{i=1}^{n} G'_i/n = \frac{\sum_{i=1}^{n} [E_i(1+p_i) - R_i]}{n}$$

$$= \frac{\Sigma E_i}{n} + \frac{\Sigma E_i P_i}{n} - \frac{\Sigma R_i}{n} = \bar{E} - \bar{R} + \bar{X}$$

where $\bar{X} = \frac{\Sigma E_i P_i}{n}$

The relative change in position is given by

$$G'_i/\bar{G}' - G_i/\bar{G} = \frac{E_i - R_i + x_i}{\bar{E} - \bar{R} + \bar{X}} - \frac{E_i - R_i}{\bar{E} - \bar{R}}$$

$$= \frac{X_i(\bar{E} - \bar{R}) - \bar{X}(E_i - R_i)}{(\bar{E} - \bar{R})(\bar{E} - \bar{R} + \bar{X})} \qquad ...(3.3)$$

From (3.3) the following condition emerges:

$G'_i/\bar{G}' \gtrless G_i/\bar{G}$ if $x_i/\bar{x} \gtrless G_i/\bar{G}$ ...(3.4)

Here the factor determining the change in the position of a State is the ratio of $x_i/\bar{x}$ relative to the ratio of $G_i/\bar{G}$. If the change in a State's expenditure relative to the average change in expenditure for all the States taken together is greater/less than the ratio of the initial grant (E_i-R_i) to the average initial grant $(\bar{E}-\bar{R})$, then it stands to gain/lose, the position of the States with $x_i/\bar{x}=G_i/\bar{G}$ remaining unchanged. The impact of an unequal proportionate decrease in expenditure (which is the same as that of an unequal proportionate increase in revenue) on the comparative grant received by a State will be opposite to that mentioned above.

$$G_i=E_i-R_i \qquad \ldots(1)$$

Expenditure of State '*i*' remains constant, its revenue raising capacity increases by a proportion q_i, so that

$$E'_i=E_i$$

$$R'_i=R_i(1+q_i)$$

Hence $G'_i=E'_i-R_i=E_i-R_i(1+q_i)=E_i-R_i-Y_i \qquad \ldots(2)$

where $Y_i=R_iq_i$

Also $\bar{G}=\Sigma G_i/n=\Sigma E_i/n-\Sigma R_i/n=\bar{E}-\bar{R}$

and $\bar{G}'=\Sigma G'_i/n=\dfrac{\Sigma(E'_i-R'_i)}{n}=\dfrac{\Sigma(E_i-R_i-Y_i)}{n}$

$$=\bar{E}-\bar{R}-\bar{Y}$$

where $\bar{Y}=\Sigma R_iq_i/n$

The change in the relative position of a State is given by

$$G'_i/\bar{G}'-G_i/\bar{G}=\frac{E_i-R_i-Y_i}{\bar{E}-\bar{R}-\bar{Y}}-\frac{E_i-R_i}{\bar{E}-\bar{R}}$$

$$=\frac{\bar{Y}(E_i-R_i)-Y_i(\bar{E}-\bar{R})}{(\bar{E}-\bar{R}-\bar{Y})(\bar{E}-\bar{R})} \qquad \ldots(3)$$

From (3) the following results follow :

$$G'_i/\bar{G}'_i \gtrless G_i/\bar{G} \text{ if } \bar{Y}/Y_i \gtrless G_i/\bar{G} \qquad \ldots(4)$$

States with a ratio of increase in its revenues to the average increase in it less/greater than the ratio of initial grant received by it to the initial average grant stand to gain/lose, the position of the States having equality between these two ratios remaining unaltered.

Model IV :

In Model II we analysed the impact of an equal (proportionate) increase in either expenditure or revenue on the comparative grant received by States. We shall now look at a more realistic situation where there is an equal (proportionate) increase in revenue and expenditure simultaneously. Let an equal increase in expenditure by a proportion 'p' in all the States be accompanied by an increase in revenue by a proportion 'q'. As in the earlier models.

$$G_i = E_i - R_i \qquad \ldots(4.1)$$

The change postulated would result in

$$E'_i = E_i(1+p)$$

$$\text{and } R'_i = R_i(1+q)$$

Therefore $\quad G'_i = E'_i - R'_i = E_i(1+p) - R_i(1+q)$[8] $\quad \ldots(4.2)$

The average grants before and after the change are defined as

$$\bar{G} = \Sigma G_i/n = (\Sigma E_i - \Sigma R_i)/n = \bar{E} - \bar{R}$$

$$\text{and} \quad \bar{G}' = \Sigma G'_i/n = \frac{\Sigma E_i(1+p) - \Sigma R_i(1+q)}{n}$$

$$= (1+p)\bar{E} - (1+q)\bar{R}$$

The relative change in the position of a State is given by

$$G'_i/\bar{G}' - G_i/\bar{G} = \frac{E_i(1+p) - R_i(1+q)}{\bar{E}(1+p) - \bar{R}(1+q)} - \frac{E_i - R_i}{\bar{E} - \bar{R}}$$

$$= \frac{(p-q)[R_i\bar{E} - E_i\bar{R}]}{[\bar{E}(1+p) - \bar{R}(1+q)][\bar{E} - \bar{R})]} \qquad \ldots(4.3)$$

From (4.3), two sets of results can be derived. The first set is under the assumption that $p > q$ *i.e.* the proportionate increase in expenditure is greater than the proportion in revenue raising capacity. In the second case, the supposition is that $p < q$.[9]

If $p > q$, then the following results hold good.

$$G'_i/\bar{G}' \gtrless G_i/\bar{G} \text{ if } \bar{E}/\bar{R} \gtrless E_i/R_i \qquad \ldots(4.4)$$

Condition (4.4) is similar to that obtained in Model II. States with a ratio of expenditure to revenue less/more than the average stand to gain/lose, the position of the States with a ratio of expenditure to revenue equal to the average ratio remaining unchanged. The identity in results with those of

Model II is because the proportionate increase in expenditure is assumed to be higher than that in the revenue and the situation converges on one where just an increase in expenditure is being considered.

If $p<q$, then

$$\frac{G'_i}{\bar{G}'} \gtrless \frac{G_i}{\bar{G}} \text{ if and only if } \frac{\bar{E}}{\bar{R}} \gtrless \frac{E_i}{R_i} \quad ...(4.5)$$

Here, the equal proportionate increase in revenues is assumed to be greater than that in expenditure so that the impact of such a change is opposite to that mentioned in the preceding paragraph.

Model V :

In this model we analyse the impact of a simultaneous (unequal proportionate) change in revenues and in expenditure on the comparative grants received by States. Here, expenditure of State 'i' increases by a proportion 'p_i' and its revenues increase by a proportion 'q_i'.

As before $G_i = E_i - R_i$ ...(1)

Expenditure and revenues of State 't' after the change is :

$E'_i = E_i(1+p_i)$ and $R'_i = R_i(1+q_i)$

$$G'_i = E'_i - R'_t = E_i(1+p_i) - R_i(1+q_i)$$
$$= E_i + x_i - R_i - y_i^{10} \quad ...(5.2)$$

Where $x_i = E_i p_i$ and $y_i = R_i q_i$

The average grant before and after the change is :

$$\bar{G} = \Sigma G_i/n = (\Sigma E_i - \Sigma R_i)/n = \bar{E} - \bar{R}$$

$$\bar{G}' = \frac{\Sigma G'_i}{n} = \frac{\Sigma(E'_i - R'_i)}{n} = \frac{\Sigma E_i + \Sigma x_i - \Sigma R_i - \Sigma y_i}{n}$$
$$= \bar{E} + \bar{x} - \bar{R} - \bar{y}$$

where $\bar{x} = \Sigma x_i/n$ and $\bar{y} = \Sigma y_i/n$

The change in the position of a State relative to the average is given by :

$$\frac{G'_i}{\bar{G}'} - \frac{G_i}{\bar{G}} = \frac{E_i + x_i - R_i - y_i}{\bar{E} + \bar{x} - \bar{R} - \bar{y}} - \frac{E_i - R_i}{\bar{E} - \bar{R}}$$

$$= \frac{(\bar{E} - \bar{R})(x_i - y_i) - (\bar{x} - \bar{y})(E_i - R_i)}{(\bar{E} + \bar{x} - \bar{R} - \bar{y})(\bar{E} - \bar{R})} \quad ...(5.3)$$

From (5.3), we have

$$G'_i/\bar{G}' \gtrless G_i/\bar{G} \text{ if } \frac{x_i - y_i}{\bar{x} - \bar{y}} \gtrless G_i/\bar{G} \qquad ..(5.4)$$

From (5.4) it follows that the impact of simultaneous (unequal proportionate) changes in expenditure and revenues of States depends on the relation between two ratios: (*i*) the ratio of net difference in its financial position to the average of the net difference for all the States, and (*ii*) the ratio of its initial grant to the average initial grant of the States taken together. States with the ratio (*i*) greater/less than the ratio, (*ii*) are better off/worse off. The position of States for which these two ratios are equal remains unaltered.

In Models I to V we have been looking at progressively more complicated situations. Model V seems to converge to reality within the framework of the assumptions of our analysis. Changes in the expenditure of a State tend to occur together with those in its revenues. Whether it stands to gain or lose by a certain change in both depends on the relative magnitude of changes in the two variables. Also, if the position of a State relative to the average is to be taken, then each variable is to be viewed in relation to its average for the entire country. All this has been brought out clearly in very simplified situations we have considered above.

In the context of empirical study, however, a number of other factors become highly significant. One such factor is the composition of the items of expenditure and of revenue of the different States. The magnitude of the grants to a State will vary according to the variation in these components. If the proportion of different items of expenditure to the total expenditure also differs as between the States, the relative grants received by them will be affected materially. The same holds good for revenue and its components. In arriving at any plausible criterion for the allocation of grants, such inter-State differences must be taken into account by adopting some basis of standardisation. In the next chapter, we shall concern ourselves primarily with one such system of standardisation and analyse its effect on the grants received by different States.

Notes and References

1 For a discussion of 'standard' expenditure and revenue see Chapter 4. These models consider the impact of a change in between the two immediate periods.

2 Assume that $G_i \geqslant 0$ so that E_i always $\geqslant R_i$.

3 Assume that $G_i \geqslant 0$ so that $E_i \geqslant R_i$.

4 All primed variables stand for the situation after the change in expenditure.

5 'n' is the number of States.

6 The expression on the right hand side of (1.3), the denominator is always positive, since by the assumption of footnote 1. $E_i > R_i$, therefore $\Sigma E_i > \Sigma R_i$, or $E_c > R_c$.

7 Note p_i is different from 'p' which was the equal proportionate change in the case of all the States.

8 Note that G_i to be > 0 $E_i (1+p) > R_i (1+q)$.

9 The general argument is again based on the condition necessary for the numerator to be positive, negative or zero to indicate the impact. The denominator, as mentioned earlier, will always be positive.

10 Note that $G_i > 0$ if and only if $E_i (1+p_i) > R_i (1+q_i)$.

4

METHODOLOGY FOR THE EMPIRICAL STUDY

THIS study suggests a technique for determining the magnitude of transfer of funds on current account from the Centre to the constituent States including all the States[1] throughout the period in the Indian Union.

According to our approach, allocation of resources on the basis of equity implies that each State is entitled to a grant representing the difference between standard expenditure and standard revenue. The procedure adopted for computing standard revenue has been discussed in Section I. The computation of standard expenditure has been done on two alternative bases as follows: The first alternative takes expenditure on each head on the basis of population and has been considered in Section II. The second alternative makes use of different appropriate characteristics for different heads of expenditure, it has been discussed in Section III. In Section IV the case for and the procedure of computing results on the basis of efficiency are given. Section V deals with sources of data and their limitations. Section VI brings out the points of differences between our study and that of Sastri.[2]

SECTION I

Standard revenue has been taken as the sum of standard tax revenue and standard non-tax revenue. In computing the former, we have worked out the results on four different bases.

This has been done to encourage increasingly the less developed States. The first basis of computation yields results favourable to States with per capita income above the average. The second, third and the fourth bases yield result favourable to less developed States as these attach increasing significance to comparative per capita income of the State by raising it to the power one, two and three respectively.[3] The first set measures tax revenue by determining the ratio of total of taxes collected by all the States to the total of their income[4] and multiplying this ratio by the income of the given State. Other bases have been measured on the lines suggested by Sastri. According to him, potential tax raising capacity can be obtained by multiplying the ratio of State tax revenue to the total income of all the States by the ratio of per capita income of the given State to the per capita income of all the States. (The latter has been raised to the power one, two and three by us to introduce increasing equitability in the scheme.) This is multiplied by the income of the State to yield uncorrected potential tax raising capacity. As however, for consistency the total of actual States' tax revenue must be equal to total of potential tax raising capacity of all the States adjustment is required to correct any surplus or deficit. This adjusting factor is the ratio of total (actual) States tax revenue to the total of uncorrected potential tax raising capacity. Thus, the corrected potential tax raising capacity for the State '*i*' is the product of its uncorrected potential tax raising capacity and the adjusting factor.

In symbols :

$$Pt_i = \frac{\Sigma STR}{\Sigma Y}\left[\frac{y_i}{\bar{y}}\right]^2 \times Y_i \qquad i = 1, 2, \ldots 15$$

$$\text{and } Pt'_i = Pt_i \times \frac{\Sigma STR}{\Sigma Pt_i}$$

where Pt_i is the uncorrected potential tax raising capacity of the State '*i*';

Pt_i' is the corrected potential tax raising capacity of the State '*i*';

ΣSTR is the sum of State tax revenue of all the States;

ΣY is the income of all the States;

Y_i is the income of the 'i'th State;

$\bar{y}$ is the average of per capita income of all the States;

y_i is the per capita income of the 'i'th State.

It may be noted that Sastri has computed potential tax raising capacity on the assumption of proportionate and moderate progression by raising $y_i/\bar{y}$ to the power two. His preference for progression is further supported by his statement that cost of collection does not increase proportionately with an increase in the taxes collected.[5]

We have worked out these additional three sets of results based on (*i*) the ratio of per capita income of the given State to the per capita income of the country which is termed the proportionate formula; (*ii*) raising the above ratio to the power two termed the formula of moderate progression; and (*iii*) raising the ratio to power three termed the formula of steeper progression to ensure balanced regional growth. The effect of progression in our approach is to inflate the standard tax revenue of the States having higher per capita income than the average (per capita income of the country) and deflate the standard tax revenue of the States with lower per capita income than the average.

The formula adopted for measuring the standard tax revenue of a State on the first basis has been extended for measuring standard expenditure. Thus, the total (actual) expenditure on the given head of States is multiplied by the ratio of number of standardizing units in the given State to its total number for all States. There is, however, a difference in computing standard expenditure; each head of expenditure is standardized individually (as given in Section III) whereas the standard tax revenue is treated on an aggregative level.

This procedure applied to expenditure can be introduced in computing standard revenue for each individual tax and the results summed up to yield the composite figure. For example, we could compute standard tax from sales tax on the basis of the turnover for the entire country. Similarly, revenue from excise duties could be standardized on the basis of the production of various commodities subject to excise duties. Likewise, revenue from agricultural income-tax could be standardized on the basis of agricultural income. This approach may have enabled us to arrive at more precise results. But the difficulties involved in procuring the requisite information will necessitate approximations which might off set the advantage of precision.[6] We have not therefore gone into this disaggregative exercise for tax revenue.

In computing standard non-tax revenue standardisation procedure is as follows : the ratio of non-tax revenue for all the States to their total revenue receipts is first calculated; it is then multiplied by the total revenue of the given State. Total non-tax revenue includes revenue from sources like public undertakings, education, medical and public health, agriculture, industry, irrigation, cooperation and so on; grants from the Centre both specific and non-specific are also included (except those under Article 275).[7]

SECTION II

Measurement of standard expenditure on the basis of population is attempted in this section. This lays stress on purely equity considerations. The procedure is as follows : average expenditure per person for the entire country is multiplied by the population of the given State. Here we have not computed expenditure on each head, that is education, health, agriculture etc. because the final composite result would not be different.[8]

SECTION III

The second alternative for measuring standard expenditure involves detailed computations for each individual head. Heads of expenditure have been classified into three groups. The first group consists of those items which have been standardized on the basis of some special characteristic and includes (*a*) education; (*b*) medical and public health; (*c*) agriculture; (*d*) industry; (*e*) irrigation; (*f*) public debt and (*g*) community development. The second group consists of those heads which are to be standardized in the same manner for the entire group and includes (*a*) tax collection; (*b*) general administration, administration of justice and jails; (*c*) police;

(*d*) animal husbandry; (*e*) cooperation; (*f*) public works; (*g*) printing and stationery; (*h*) pensions and (*i*) forests. The third group consists of items which are classified as miscellaneous and includes those heads of expenditure which have not been covered under the previous two groups, for example, labour and employment, electricity, development of miscellaneous organisations and so on; and the items which are peculiar to various States. Such items do not recur from year to year. Considering the unpredictable nature of the changes in these items standard expenditure has been taken at its given level.

The technique for computing standard expenditure on items included in the first group consists in calculating the average cost per standard unit for the entire country[9] and multiplying this by the actual number of standard units in the given State. For example, standard expenditure on education is arrived at by calculating average expenditure per student for different levels of education and multiplying this by the actual number of students in the given State. Similarly, expenditure on medical and public health, agriculture, industry, irrigation, debt charges and community development has been standardized on the bases of population, net cropped area, number of persons employed in Government factories, net irrigated area, average of the loans outstanding at the beginning and at the end of the year and population respectively. The underlying assumptions are (*i*) that for the country as a whole actual expenditure implies efficient utilization of resources and (*ii*) the present level of service does not call for any improvement. In connection with the first assumption, it may be stated that a certain amount of waste is almost inevitable in any kind of expenditure. So, the norm of standard expenditure may imply a given degree of inefficient utilization. The second assumption can, however, be removed[10] if the degree of improvement to be made in the provision of a particular service over its present all-India level is given in quantitative terms. Standard expenditure on various heads can then be adjusted accordingly.

In computing standard expenditure on education, the standard unit is the number of students in a State. For this purpose, expenditure on education has been divided into five parts, viz. (*i*) university level, (*ii*) secondary education level, (*iii*) primary level, (*iv*) special education and (*v*) expenditure on administration of education. The standard expenditure on students belonging to first group has been computed by ascertaining the average cost per student for all the States belonging to this group and multiplying this by actual number of students in the given State in that stage. The same formula has been adopted for the next three groups. Expenditure on administration of education consisting of direction and superintendence has been standardized on the basis of total number of students on rolls.

One of the limitations of this approach of standardisation is that it has not taken account of differences in the pay scales of teachers in different States, which would have required the multiplication of the standard expenditure by the ratio of average pay scales for all the States to the pay scales of the given State. This exercise has not been carried out owing to non-availability of data for all the years. Another limitation of this approach relates to the fact that if for a State the standard expenditure on education is greater than actual expenditure, the concerned State may not be able to utilize the transferred fund because the number of persons who can be enrolled as students cannot increase[11] as this is a function of a number of variables e.g. (*i*) age composition of population, (*ii*) level of economic development of the State, (*iii*) the means of transportation, (*iv*) density of population and so on. This problem is not likely to arise in the present context in India where we have very low levels of education and heavy population pressure.

Standard expenditure on medical and public health has been computed by calculating average cost on medical and public health per thousand persons in all the States and multiplying this by the actual population of the given State. It must be admitted that computation of standard expenditure on the basis of number of doctors or hospital beds (a worse index than the former) could also have been considered; since medical facilities may exist in the absence of hospitals, say, in the form of out-patient dispensaries and since data on hospital beds and doctors where available were not comprehensive, this exercise has not been attempted.

Expenditure on agriculture consists of costs of improvement of seeds, agricultural engineering, experimental farms, marketing and so on. In our approach, we have standardized expenditure on agriculture on the basis of net cropped area. Net and not gross cropped area has been taken on the assumption that expenditure on agriculture is a function of an increase in the physical area under agriculture and not of an increase in double cropping. Thus, in the first instance, we obtain average cost of expenditure per thousand acres for all the States and multiply this by the actual net cropped area in the given State. Another basis of standardisation can be the number of persons employed in agriculture on the analogy of standardising procedure for expenditure on industry. This exercise has not been undertaken on account of unreliability of the data.

Expenditure on industry includes that on industrial development, marketing and industrial training schools etc. and we have adopted number of persons employed in government factories as the basis of standardisation. Thus we compute average cost per person employed in government factories by dividing total expenditure on industry of all the States by the number of persons employed in these factories. This average multiplied by the actual number of persons employed in government factories in the given State yields standard expenditure. It may be mentioned that capital employed in various industrial units can be another basis of standardisation but we have not adopted this on account of the conceptual difficulties involved in measuring capital.[12]

Standard expenditure on irrigation has been computed on the basis of net area irrigated. An important point to note in this context is that there are different sources of providing irrigational facilities. The cost of providing irrigational facilities per thousand acres from wells is different from natural lakes or from multipurpose projects. The last source will raise further complications regarding allocation of costs among various heads. We have, in our approximation, abstracted from these problems.

Expenditure on debt charges is the sum of interest charged and appropriations for reduction or avoidance of debt. The interest charged in its own turn is net of the amount debited to various departments making use of these funds. The net figure for interest charges is negative for some of the States.[13] To overcome the difficulty involved in computing standard expenditure on interest charges and appropriations separately, we have standardized expenditure on debt charges (interest charges and appropriations) on the basis of the average of loans outstanding at the beginning and at the end of the year.[14] Thus standard expenditure on debt charges has been computed by multiplying average cost of debt charges for the entire country (obtained by dividing debt charges incurred by all the States by the total of average loans outstanding of these States) by the actual average loans outstanding for the given State. It is necessary to note that there are certain other difficulties in computing standard expenditure on debt charges. In the first instance, rates of interest payable on the different loans raised by States vary. Also, they have different periods of maturity. Computation of average rate of interest or average period of maturity is in itself an approximation. However, on the assumption that rates of interest offered by the different States on loans raised at the same time are equal, this approach is quite meaningful. But the rates of interest offered by different States as also the same State, in respect of loans raised at different points of time are different and this introduces complications.

Expenditure on community development was meant to uplift the standard of living of the people living in rural areas, through the provision of rural electrification, irrigational facilities, development of roads and so on. A proper basis of standardisation in this case is the effort made by the people to uplift their own lot because the contribution by the Centre was to be on a basis matching the effort made by the people of rural area. Since it is not possible to have a quantitative measure of the effort made by the people belonging to a given State we have computed standard expenditure on the basis of population. This assumes, of course, that the effort made is proportional to population.

For computing standard expenditure of items in the second group the basis is the same for all the items covered in the group. The ratio of expenditure on the given head to the total revenue expenditure incurred by all the States is first ascertained. This ratio multiplied by the actual total revenue expenditure of the given State yields standard expenditure on the given item. The alternative technique of computing standard expenditure on the basis of some special characteristic has not been applied in view of the fact that expenditure on items included under this group does not constitute a significant percentage of total revenue expenditure and the final conclusions would not have been affected much. Besides, some of the items included in this group are such as do not suggest any appropriate basis for computing standard expenditure. For example, in the case of expenditure on cooperation and public works it is not very clear which characteristic is appropriate for standardisation.

As mentioned earlier, expenditure on items included in the third group under the heading miscellaneous has been taken at their actual values. No procedure of standardisation has been adopted in this case because most of the expenditure on items included in the head miscellaneous are special to various States. Some of the items covered under this head include expenditure on State statistics, presentation and translation of ancient manuscripts, donations for charitable purposes, special Commissions of Enquiry, irrevocable temporary loans, grants-in-aid and contributions and so on, charges in connection with village Panchayat Acts, expenditure on displaced persons, flood reliefs, National Emergency and so on. It must be mentioned that expenditure on miscellaneous items put together comes to a significant amount in the case of most of the States. But, since the items are of a heterogeneous nature, standardisation is not possible and has not been attempted.

SECTION IV

Having computed standard revenue and standard expenditure, the grant that each State is entitled to is given by the difference between the two. It may be recalled that we have computed standard tax revenue on four different bases and standard expenditure on two different bases. As a consequence, we have got eight sets of magnitudes of transfer from the Centre to the States. All these sets of results are discouraging to the economically advanced States for example Punjab, Maharashtra and Gujarat. To avoid or minimise the penalising of States that make an effort to increase their incomes the results[15] have been multiplied by certain weights calculated to give a bias in favour of more 'efficient' States. The weight given to a State in a given year 'i' is the ratio of the change in State income in the year under consideration relative to the previous year divided by the income of the previous year. This system of weighting[16] leads to another four sets of results favourable to more efficient States. I may point out that one of the drawbacks of such an exercise relates to the underlying assumption that an increase in the income of the State is the result of an effort made by the State. Another is that an increased expenditure by the State Government may tend to increase its income through multiplier effect.

It is possible that for some States the resultant figure of transfer of funds from the Centre may be negative. This will imply that the State concerned ought not to get any grant, and further, this negative figure gives an approximate measure of the extra benefit enjoyed by it. Note that such a situation will be interpreted, by the approach as given by Musgrave,[17] to mean that such a State must refund this amount to the Centre. According to our approach, it will imply the absence of a central grant. This arises out of the postulation of a unilateral flow of funds. It may be noted that by assuming a unilateral flow of grants, this approach implicitly encourages efforts to raise the level of State taxation (because it does not reduce the magnitude of transfer from the Centre). However, this incentive is present only for those States whose standard revenue is greater than standard expenditure.

So far the approach of this study assumes that the resources of the Centre are infinitely elastic and can meet the requirements of all the States to any extent. If this assumption was to be given up and the total amount of desired transfers to different States is to be equal to the total of actual transfers a correction is required. This correcting factor is the ratio of total of actual transfers to all the States to the total of desired transfers of these States. The results of these modified desired transfers to different States are given in the appendix.[18] It will be seen that the results are not materially different from those obtained earlier.

SECTION V

Sources of data and their limitations

In this section we evaluate the authenticity of the sources of information and bring to focus the steps taken to ensure comparability both between the States and over the period of study. Both the problems are important in the present context because the data used refer to fifteen States and the period of study ranges from 1957-58 to 1980-81 (including the period of projection). Further, because of the nature of data some assumptions have crept into the analysis. We shall examine how far these assumptions limit the usefulness of our study.

The information used has been mainly on two aspects. First relates to the data of State-wise expenditure and revenue (tax and non-tax) and is the mainstay of our empirical study. Second refers to the units used to compute standard revenue and standardize expenditure on various heads.

Data on revenue from State taxes, non-tax sources and actual transfers as per the recommendations of various Finance Commissions has been taken from budgets.[19] Computation of standard tax requires information on both the per capita income and the total income of each State. The Central Statistical Organisation has adjusted the information furnished by State Statistical Bureaus and brought it out in mimeographed form.[20] Income (per capita as well as total) has been given at both current and constant prices. We have used income at current prices in our computation since information on State tax revenue (which is one of the variables) is at current prices.

The basic source of material relating to expenditure on various heads is the budgets of States.[21] Data on actual amount spent in each year under different heads has been taken into account. Information on number of students is available in two publications, one issued by the Ministry of Education and the other by the respective State Bureaus.[22] We use the first source as the Ministry of Education adjusts the information furnished by different States to bring it to a comparable basis. This publication is available up to the year 1962-63. For subsequent years, we have used the unpublished data computed by the Ministry of Education.[23]

The next item of expenditure is medical and public health. An exercise adopting the number of doctors as the unit of standardisation was conducted in this case. Digest of Health Statistics[24] did not give a complete time series over the period of study. The State statistical bureaus, on the other hand, did not publish their Abstracts regularly for all the years. Considering these difficulties population was adopted as the basis of standardisation. The data on population was obtained from the Report of the Registrar General.[25] Expenditure on community development was also standardized on the basis of population.

Information on net cropped area, which is the basis of computing standard expenditure on agriculture, is available from two different sources.[26] The Ministry of Food and Agriculture makes some adjustment in the data published in its mimeographed publication and hence our preference for this source.

Number of persons employed in Government factories is the basis for computing standard expenditure on industry. Information on this is contained in two publications of the Ministry of Labour and Employment[27] and also in the Statistical Abstracts of the States. For completeness and uniformity, we once again prefer the data published by the Central Ministry.

Information on net irrigated area is also taken from the mimeographed publication of Ministry of Food and Agriculture.[28] As earlier, this Central source was preferred to the Statistical Abstracts published by the State Bureaus.

Information on the average of the loans outstanding in the beginning and at the end of the year is obtained from the

State budgets. There is no chance of a discrepancy between the information published in the State budgets and Statistical Abstracts, but the irregular publication of Statistical Abstracts has prompted us to concentrate on State budgets for the statistical data on loans outstanding.

SECTION VI

Sastri starts with a given amount of divisible pool and provides a procedure for allocating this among different States. We, on the other hand, compute the amount of desired transfer independently for each State which ultimately determines the amount of desired pool.

Sastri makes use of the potential tax raising capacity to arrive at the figure of maladjustment. In our study, potential tax raising capacity is calculated to determine the total revenue (the difference between standard expenditure and standard revenue measures the desired transfer).

Notes and References

1 Excluding Union Territories and Nagaland (hereafter referred to as all States).

2 K.V.S. Sastri, *Ibid.*

3 Given the magnitude of divergence between the per capita income of the 'i'th state and the average, and the number of years over which it is to be eliminated, one can work out the different values to which this ratio has to be raised for different States. This technique would have necessitated making assumptions regarding rate of growth and the time horizon over which these inequalities are to be eliminated which dissuaded us from carrying out this exercise.

4 It may he noted that the ratio of Income of Union Territories to the total National Income varies from 8.9 per cent to 9.5 per cent.

5 Sastri has proved mathematically the relationship between cost of tax collection and tax revenue raised. He reaches the conclusion that the cost of tax collection increases less than proportionately to the tax revenue.

6 For instance, it is difficult to get an idea about the agricultural income and its State-wise break-down. Similarly the turnover of products and its aggregation will necessitate assumptions regarding the weightage to be attached to each product.

7 This has been done because the magnitude of desired transfer (as computed by us) represents total transfer (on current account) including that under Article 275.

8 If the results of standard expenditure on different items were to be compared, computation for the individual components will be more meaningful.

9 Excluding Nagaland and Union Territories.

10 We have not computed the results of projections on the basis of different levels of improvement in providing different services for the reasons mentioned in Chapter 6 on Projections

11 This limitation was pointed out by Dr. B.V. Krishnamurthy during the course of a discussion with him.

12 The composition of number of persons employed in Government and non-Government factories in different States is not markedly different.

13 This is applicable to Andhra Pradesh and Punjab.

14 $L_A = \frac{L_B + L_E}{2}$, where L_A stands for average of the loans outstanding; L_B for loans outstanding in the beginning of the year and L_E for loans outstanding at the end of the year.

15 We have computed the results based on efficiency only for those sets when standard expenditure is computed on the basis of appropriate yardsticks for each item. The results of sets based on population have not been considered because these were obtained on the extreme assumption of equity.

16 Note that we have also calculated the weights for efficiency on the basis of (i) change in per capita income and (ii) tax effort as a percentage of its income for each State.

17 R.A. Musgrave, *Op. cit.*, f.n. 3 of Chapter 1.

18 See Statistical Tables 5.1, 5.2 and 5.3.

19 Government of different States, *State Budgets*, for different years.

20 Government of India, Central Statistical Organisation : *Estimates of Total and Per Capita Net Domestic Product for Different States as Prepared and Published/Cleared for Publication by the Respective State Governments*. It may be noted that the Report of Fifth Finance Commission has also published information on these heads (Per Capita and State Income) quoting the same source (i.e. C.S.O.), but the figures differ on account of methodology used in computing income. We have used data given by C.S.O. for maintaining uniformity.

21 *Ibid.*, f.n. 19.

22 Government of India, Ministry of Education, *Education in States*, for various years. Governments of different States, Statistical Bureaus, *Statistical Abstracts* (different States) for various years.

23 Government of India, Ministry of Education, *Provisional Statistics of Education in States*, for various years.

24 Government of India, Ministry of Health: *Digest of Health Statistics.*

25 Government of India, *Report of the Registrar General on Population.*

26 Government of India, Ministry of Food and Agriculture : *Summary of Statistics Relati g to Agric ulture* and the *Statistical Abstracts* of the States.

27 Government of India, Ministry of Labour Employment : *Digest of Labour Statistics* and *Labour Year Book* for different years.

28 *Ibid.*, f.n. 26.

5

ANALYSIS OF EMPIRICAL RESULTS

IN this Chapter we present an analysis of results computed on the basis of the methodology outlined in Chapter 4. The results have been worked out in three stages. In stage one standard expenditure has been normalised on the basis of population and standard tax revenue has been calculated introducing very high significance to relative per capita income. It is obvious that these results are favourable to poor states with high population. This procedure, therefore, should be used if the objective of the government is to foster balanced regional growth and remove disparities in the level of services provided by different states.

Stage two results have been computed by calculating standard expenditure capturing individual characteristics of different heads of expenditure as outlined in Chapter 4. In these results standard tax revenue does not assign any weightage to relative per capita income. As a result, these recommendations on desired transfer are favourable to rich states with developed level of socio-economic infrastructure. If the objective of the resource disbursing authority is to encourage relatively rich states, guided by considerations of efficiency, then these results provide useful information. Note that these results attach moderate degree of significance to efficient states.

Stage three results are most favourable to rich states who are consistent in their tax effort and/or make a special effort leading to a rise in their state's income. Tax effort, of course, depends upon the individual efforts of the states. For example, the more efficient a state is in realising the tax proceeds, the higher is the proportion of tax revenue to the income of the state. However, a state may be able to raise a higher proportion of its income as tax by raising the rates of tax. At times, a higher tax effort my be an outcome of the state resorting to regressive taxation and it is somewhat debatable whether such states need to be encouraged by transferring additional resources out of the common pool. The criterion of change in state's income over the previous year, to identify efficient states presupposes that the income of any state is an outcome of policies followed by it. This may be true to a limited degree. It is true that a state may be able to attract potential investors by offering them incentives. This may lead to a rise in its income. However, if a state is handicapped due to topographical and climatic factors, it may be able to achieve a marginal increase in its income.

Despite these limitations stage three results are obtained as the product of stage two results and the efficiency parameter. Efficiency parameter is given by $\triangle Y_i / Y_i\,(t-1)$. This gives the measure of absolute efficiency. It is normalised by finding the ratio of A_i to sum of A_i where A_i is the absolute measure of efficiency for individual states.

This chapter is divided into three sections. In Section I, we analyse the results of first stage which are guided by considerations of equality. Section II presents an analysis of stage two results where the objective of the fiscal authorities is to assign moderate degree of credit to rich states. Section III presents the findings of the exercises that attach added significance to efficiency of states as given by consistency in their (i) tax effort and (ii) income.

The period of study extends from 1957-58 to 1976-77. No doubt there has been a reorganisation of States and therefore the results are strictly comparable up to 1970-71. To economise on space we present the results of five different points in time 1957-58, 1961-62, 1964-65, 1967-68 and 1976-77. We hope that this range of results shall be able to present a wide choice to decision-making body. As discussed in Chapter 6 these results can be used in assessing whether the allocation of resources to different states has been fair.

SECTION I

The results of first stage, which are favourable to poor and less developed states, indicate that states can be classified into three groups : (a) those which received an amount less than the desired transfer at all the points of study, (b) those which received an amount more than the desired transfer at all the points of reference, and (c) those for which the results present a mixed picture--in some year/s the actual transfer was less than the desired transfer and in others the actual transfer was more than the desired transfer. As was expected the heavily populated poor states Bihar, Madhya Pradesh and Uttar Pradesh fall in the first category. The second category includes states (i) which are of strategic importance to the country—Assam and Jammu & Kashmir, (ii) rich states—Gujarat, Maharashtra, Punjab, Haryana and Karnataka and (iii) the relatively newly formed states of Himachal Pradesh, Meghalaya and Tripura. The third category includes states for which results are not uniform—Andhra Pradesh, Kerala, Orissa, Rajasthan, Tamil Nadu and West Bengal. It is possible to restrict the exercise by indicating whether the desired transfer was more or less than the actual. Alternatively, we identify the extent of divergence between the desired transfer and the actual transfer. This part of the exercise is particularly significant to States. Besides, actual transfer being less than the desired in a year may be compensated by its being more than the desired transfer in other year/s. However, this poses a problem of adding the quantum of divergence of resources accruing at different points in time. This necessitates the computation of present value of extent of divergence corresponding to different points in time and has been attempted in this study. From the point of view of political analyses it may have different implications. For example, the actual transfer may be more than the desired

TABLE 5.1 : **The results of desired transfer from the centre to various states (Stage One)**

(*Rs. lakhs*)

States	1957-58		1961-62		1964-65		1967-68		1976-77	
	Desired	Actual	Desired	Actual	Desired	Actual	Desired	Actual	Desired	Actual
1. Andhra Pradesh	1457	1407	2978	1975	2547	3080	6372	4657	23381	25125
2. Assam	—435	775	191	965	529	1466	667	2883	11422	14749
3. Bihar	5289	1589	8125	2130	11110	2620	NA	—	55060	18452
4. Gujarat	—	—	—207	1860	—180	2138	965	2386	—18195	8299
5. Jammu & Kashmir	175	445	—106	498	152	529	24	1295	1004	8663
6. Karnataka	143	1241	630	1557	1260	2045	2857	4320	9044	10868
7. Kerala	983	611	1385	825	1256	1717	2524	3736	7071	11527
8. Madhya Pradesh	1660	1121	2496	1569	3562	2184	8095	3188	35208	19372
9. Maharashtra	—771	1988	—3022	1582	—7253	3070	—4975	5202	—74405	23814
10. Orissa	1709	787	2020	1024	2657	2528	4412	4605	17178	8610
11. Punjab	—1943	779	—2597	1144	—7707	1483	—10055	1133	—47985	5649
12. Rajasthan	554	764	1045	1045	2160	1764	4365	2573	14505	13934
13. Tamil Nadu	525	990	274	1563	689	2326	1081	4137	21899	12503
14. Uttar Pradesh	3662	1975	9845	3172	9892	3747	20792	7362	67581	27208
15. West Bengal	—123	1590	1205	2174	2735	2178	6129	4600	14442	15123
16. Haryana	These States were not formed.								—15771	6301
17. Himachal Pradesh									—91	7235
18. Meghalaya									984	3698
19. Tripura									1236	5238

transfer when the same political party was in power as at the Centre and less when other party was at the helm of affairs. In this exercise we have not gone into these aspects. We feel that the Finance Commission makes recommendations and these are in force for five years. Thus, unless the change in political power in a state or states coincides with the setting up of the Finance Commission, this point may have very limited significance.

States for which the desired transfer is more than the actual transfer

There is a secular rise in the difference between the desired transfer and the actual transfer, in the case of all the states falling in this category, over a period of time. Recall that Bihar, Madhya Pradesh and Uttar Pradesh belong to this group. This phenomenon of growing difference between the desired transfer and the actual transfer is explicable. Population in these states increased at a rate faster than the increased transfer of resources from the Centre. Also, the per capita income of these states is less than the average for the country and hence standard tax revenue decreased due to higher weightage assigned to relative per capita income in computing standard tax revenue.

What may be influence of lack of resources on the welfare of a State ? In theory, it is argued that the more the resources available to a state, the higher is its welfare. The significance attached to the relationship between resources and welfare is so strong and well-established that the two are treated as synonyms. We would like to ponder over the nature of relationship. For example, (a) non-availability of resources from the Centre may induce a State to work harder and generate its own funds and (b) the effect on welfare shall depend upon how these resources are used. The first has a favourable influence from the point of view of the country though one could argue that with the augmented resources from the Centre, the State would have done better. The second effect may mean loss of welfare if the resources were to be allocated over useful public goods. However, if these resources were to be frittered away on non-development heads to appease people or to bolster the image of the state government, the net effect on loss of welfare may not be very strong. We are somewhat apprehensive about the final use of resources. It is quite possible that the allocation pattern of resources is influenced crucially by the relative strength of the ruling party. If the party enjoys a strong position it will not have to resort to cheap policies of winning the support of people. Also, it may not be unduly concerned about the closeness or otherwise of elections.

Bihar

Whatever the effect on welfare, the difference between the desired transfer and actual transfer grew from Rs. 37 crores in 1957-58 to Rs. 366 crores in 1976-77 in the case of Bihar. Of course, part of this increase is illusory. But the ten-fold increase in the quantum of fall in desired resources from the actual cannot be ascribed to the increase in the price level. Note that if we compute the present value of these additional resources in the year 1976-77 it would become a staggering amount. Even otherwise, an objective analysis would suggest the need to provide additional resources to these relatively poor states.

Madhya Pradesh

There is a secular increase in the difference between the desired and the actual transfer. It grew from Rs. 5.39 crores in 1957-58 to Rs. 158.36 crores. In this case the difference is particularly strong in the year 1976-77. Note that the difference in the transfers has already become about ten-fold by the year 1967-68. The difference in the transfers at different points of study were Rs. 5.39 crores, Rs. 9.27 crores, Rs. 13.78 crores, Rs. 49.07 crores and Rs. 158.36 crores. We are aware that the results may be influenced by the choice of reference years but the original study obtained information for all years and the complexion of the findings does not differ significantly.

Uttar Pradesh

The difference between the desired and the actual transfer is more pronounced in this case. It grew from Rs. 16.87 crores to Rs. 403.73 crores. This represents an alarming situation. But these results have been arrived at by attaching maximum significance to population. However, it is debatable whether monetary disincentives may induce the state to resort to implementing the policies and measures of family planning with a greater vigour. The results of next section shall mark a dramatic change in the difference between the desired and the actual transfer. Thus, in the final analysis the decision centres on the objective which the Centre seeks to achieve.

States for which the desired transfer is less than the actual transfer

These states have been allocated resources more than the desired transfer. This may have caused them to be less particular in raising the resources through their own effort. But the states of Assam, Jammu & Kashmir, Meghalaya and Tripura are of strategic importance and given the topography of these States additional resources need to be allocated to them to enable them to provide the same level of infra-structural facilities.

Assam

The desired allocation for Assam was negative in 1957-58. The actual transfer exceeded the desired transfer (referred to as difference for brevity) by Rs. 7.74 crores, Rs. 9.37 crores, Rs. 22.16 crores and Rs. 32.27 crores. This secular rise in the difference, measured in constant prices, shall provide moderate estimates of the difference.

Gujarat

The desired transfer was negative at all the points of study except the year 1967-68. These results are not startling in as much as high significance is attached to relative per capita income. Besides, it is not a state with population above the average. These factors taken simultaneously result in desired transfer yielding a negative value.

Jammu & Kashmir

The desired transfer for the year 1961-62 was negative. In other years the difference was as follows: Rs. 2.40 crores, Rs. 3.77 crores, Rs. 12.71 crores and Rs. 76.59 crores. Except for the last year of study 1976-77 the difference in the amount allocated is not very high. As mentioned earlier, the strategic importance of the state requires special importance to be paid to meet its requirements.

Karnataka

This state falls in this group by a strange coincidence. However, there is no secular rise in the difference of resources allocated to it. The difference varies from Rs. 11.98 crores to Rs. 18.24 crores from 1957-58 to 1976-77. Measured in constent prices the difference has fallen over time.

Maharashtra and Punjab

These are the two richest states and their desired allocation is negative at all the points of study. Their relatively per capita income raises their standard tax to such an extent that it exceeds standard expenditure. Besides, the procedure of actual transfers assigns some weightage to collection. Also, there is no provision for not allocating any amount to any States. The factors taken simultaneously are responsible for the present state of affairs. What is somewhat disturbing, however, is the fact that the actual transfer to Maharashtra in absolute terms is the third highest.

Haryana, Himachal Pradesh, Meghalaya and Tripura

We have not calculated the results of desired transfer for the earlier years because of non-availability of data Some of these states were formed in the early seventies. Strictly speaking, the results are valid for comparative analysis only up to the year 1967-68. Since then the reorganisation of States vitiates the comparative analysis.

States for which results are not uniform during the period of study

The results without normalisation for computing the present value of difference between the desired and the actual transfer suggest that fall in actual transfer is neutralised by rise in actual transfer at other point/s in time.

On the whole, Andhra Pradesh should have received slightly higher allocation. The desired allocation exceeded the actual transfer in 1957-58, 1961-62 and in 1967-68 by Rs. 5 crores, Rs. 10.03 crores and Rs. 17.15 crores. However, the desired transfer fell short of the actual transfer in 1967-68 and 1976-77 by Rs. 5.33 crores and Rs. 17.44 crores.

Kerala, on the whole, seems to have received an amount more than its desired transfer. This is particularly true for the year 1976-77 when the desired transfer exceeded the actual transfer by Rs. 44.56 crores. In fact, the trend of actual transfer exceeding the desired transfer started from 1964-65 and it seems to persist.

Orissa

A relatively poor State, is more akin to states like Bihar, Madhya Pradesh and Uttar Pradesh. Except for the year 1967-68 the desired transfer exceeds the actual transfer. In 1976-77, the difference is of the order of Rs. 85.68 crores which is very high.

Rajasthan

There is no uniform pattern for Rajasthan. However, on the whole, the desired transfer exceeds the actual transfer.

Tamil Nadu

The desired transfer is less than the actual transfer at all the points of study except 1976-77. In the last year of the study the desired transfer exceeds the actual transfer by Rs. 13.96 crores.

West Bengal

The difference in transfers has been fluctuating over the period of study and on the whole it balances. Even the computation of present value of differences of transfer shall not make a significant difference.

SECTION II

In this section we analyse the results where standard expenditure has been calculated incorporating special characteristics of heads of expenditure and standard tax revenue is computed by excluding relative per capita income as one of the determinants. Therefore, the results of this section, on *a priori* considerations, are expected to be favourable to rich states with highly developed level of infrastructure. The states can be divided into two groups on the basis of the results of this section. Group one includes states for which desired transfer is less than the actual transfer at all the points of study. Group two includes states for which the results are not uniform. There is no group of states for which the desired transfer is more than the actual transfer at all the points of study.

States for which the desired transfer is less than the actual

This group includes Assam, Gujarat, Karnataka, Haryana, Himachal Pradesh, Meghalaya and Tripura. Recall that, in the previous section States of J. & K., Maharashtra and Punjab also belonged to this group. The change in the procedure of computing standard tax revenue in particular is responsible for the change.

The position of Assam, Meghalaya and Tripura is understandable given their strategic location. The presence of Gujarat, Karnataka and Haryana is somewhat disturbing. These are relatively rich states and the exclusion of relative per capita income as one of the determinants of standard tax revenue should have raised the desired transfer above the level of actual transfers. Equally serious is the omission of Jammu & Kashmir from this group of states. As was expected, states of Maharashtra and Punjab now belong to the other group for which the results are not uniform.

TABLE 5.2 : **The results of desired transfer from the centre to various states (Stage Two)**

(*Rs. lakhs*)

States	1957-58		1961-62		1964-65		1967-68		1976-77	
	Desired	Actual	Desired	Actual	Desired	Actual	Desired	Actual	Desired	Actual
1. Andhra Pradesh	806	1407	1434	1975	984	3080	4729	4657	8378	25125
2. Assam	136	775	432	965	799	1466	1669	2883	4814	14749
3. Bihar	1374	1589	1461	2130	791	2620	N.A.	N.A.	26423	18452
4. Gujarat	—	—	779	1869	139	2138	2016	2380	3388	8299
5. Jammu & Kashmir	153	445	106	498	951	529	1321	1295	637	8663
6. Karnataka	570	1241	796	1557	1154	2045	1652	4320	8715	10868
7. Kerala	1053	611	1009	825	771	1717	692	3736	9302	11527
8. Madhya Pradesh	332	1121	386	1569	523	2184	3986	3188	16611	19372
9. Maharashtra	2458	1938	2045	1582	1864	3070	1877	5202	1309	23814
10. Orissa	580	787	2428	1024	1782	2528	3500	4605	7119	8610
11. Punjab	306	779	1173	1144	689	1483	275	1133	—3888	5649
12. Rajasthan	144	764	873	1045	1728	1764	4204	2573	11107	13934
13. Tamil Nadu	651	990	1224	1563	1630	2326	4312	4137	11688	12503
14. Uttar Pradesh	1702	1975	3554	3172	3191	3747	8003	7362	30590	27208
15. West Bengal	2442	1590	2134	2174	2178	2414	3969	4600	4922	15123
16. Haryana									749	6301
17. Himachal Pradesh									—1945	7235
18. Meghalaya									—2640	3698
19. Tripura									—3080	5238

The desired transfer to Assam exceeded the actual transfer by about Rs. 5 to 12 crores till 1967-68. Considering the importance of the state this is not very startling. But in 1976-77 the desired transfer exceeded the actual by about Rs. 100 crores.

As mentioned earlier, it is strange that introduction of individual characteristics to standardise expenditure did not make any difference to the desired transfer to Gujarat. Possibly, the state provides public services of a superior quality though the number of standardising units is not very large. This results in standard expenditure being not of a very high magnitude. As in the case of Assam the difference between desired and actual transfer is of a very high order for 1976-77.

Karnataka deserved an amount less than the actual transfer but there is no secular trend in the difference between the desired and the actual transfer. The difference reached the peak during 1967-68 (Rs. 26.68 crores) but declined to Rs. 21.53 crores for the year 1976-77. The change in the procedure of computing standard expenditure and standard revenue has not caused any significant difference to the gap between the desired and the actual transfers.

Of the relatively newly constituted states, the desired transfer yields a positive value only for Haryana. In the case of other states: Himachal Pradesh, Meghalaya and Tripura the desired transfer yields a negative value. Note that the desired transfer yields a negative value under the first approach for Haryana and Himachal Pradesh.

States for which the results are not uniform during the entire period of study

The desired transfer to Andhra Pradesh is less than the actual except in the year 1967-68. But the magnitude of the difference is not very high—it is around Rs. 6 crores. The year 1967-68 yields a marginal excess of desired transfer over the actual. For the terminal year of the study, this difference gives a staggering amount which may be due to very special circumstances prevailing in that year. In fact, the actual transfer is of a very high order—Rs. 251 crores.

The desired transfer to Bihar is less than the actual at all the points of study except the terminal year—1976-77. In the earlier years the desired transfer fell short of the actual by a small amount varying from Rs. 2 to Rs. 18 crores. But in 1976-77 its desired transfer exceeds actual by a staggering sum of Rs. 80 crores. Thus, in the overall position Bihar has received less than its desired transfer.

The actual transfers to Jammu & Kashmir are more less fair till the year 1967-68. The s ortfall of the desired transfers in the first two points of study is compensated by its excess during the next two points of study. The year 1976-77 however marks a dramatic change and the desired transfer falls short of the actual by about Rs. 90 crores. There has been no significant difference in the final outcome of the relationship between actual and desired transfer of this section and the previous section.

Kerala deserved an amount more than actual in the first two points of study. This pattern changed since then. But there is no secular pattern in the difference between the desired and actual transfers. On the whole, however, the desired transfer is less than the actual.

Madhya Pradesh belongs to this group only because of the year 1967-68 when the desired transfer exceeds the actual by about Rs. 8 crores. In other years its desired transfer is less than the actual. However, this amount varies from Rs. 8 to Rs. 28 crores.

Maharashtra's actual transfer is less than the desired at the first two points of study. Since then there is a secular increase in the difference between the desired and the actual transfer. There is a spectacular increase in the difference during the 1976-77. In fact it is the highest difference for any individual state. Since, actual transfer is partly guided by actual realisation from different states, it tends to inflate the value of actual transfer. This, in turn, results in the growing difference between the desired and the actual transfer.

The desired transfer is less than the actual at all the points of study except 1961-62. The magnitude of the difference is not very high and varies from Rs. 2 to Rs. 12 crores. Without discounting for time, the state appears to have received more than the desired transfer by Rs. 20 crores.

Punjab belongs to this group of states only because its desired transfer exceeds actual by Rs. 29 lakhs in the year 1961-62. In other years, the actual transfers exceed the desired transfer. However, the extent of divergence is not very significant. For the last point of study its standard revenue exceeds standard expenditure suggesting that it is not entitled to any transfer.

Rajasthan received more than the desired transfer at all the points of study except 1967-68. In that year its desired transfer exceds the actual by about Rs. 16 crores. On the whole there is not any significant divergence between the desired and the actual transfer.

Like Rajasthan, Tamil Nadu received more than its desired transfer at all the points of study except 1967-68. In other years, the actual transfer exceeds the desired by a marginal amount varying from Rs. 3 to 8 crores.

The results are somewhat unexpected for the state of Uttar Pradesh. The desired transfer exceeds the actual at three points of study. However, the magnitude of this difference is not very high except for the year 1976-77. These results suggest that the relatively poor state of U.P. should have been allocated more resources than it actually received. The probable explanation for the actual transfers falling short of the desired transfer is the poor tax collection effort of the State. Otherwise, it is a state with above average population and therefore the procedure for allocation would have resulted in raising the value of actual transfers. These exercises would recommend that the state should receive a better deal than it has hitherto.

Except in the year 1957-58, West Bengal received more than the desired transfer. However, the magnitude of this difference is not very high. The year 1976-77, however, marks a departure. In this year the desired transfer is relatively low because of a relatively high magnitude of standard tax revenue. Note that in absolute terms this state's income is the third highest in the country. Besides, actual transfers are partly guided by tax collections. This state possibly cannot argue that it has been discriminated against in the allocation of resources.

SECTION III

In this section, we present in brief the results of stage three. Recall that these results attach some weightage to effort of the state in raising its (i) income, and (ii) tax effort. There is a marginal difference to the change in the desired allocation. It does not lead to any change in the composition of the groups into which states have been classified. For the change in the desired transfer see Table 5.3.

For a quick comparison of the results (stage one, stage two and stage three) see Table 5.4.

In the next chapter we take up the question of a comparison of actual transfers with the desired transfer using different methodologies. To retain the strict validity of comparisons the results have been worked out up to the year 1967-68 and only tentative results for 1976-77 are presented. Note that a major reorganisation of the states was undertaken in the early seventies. This distorts the comparison of results over time. We feel that Chapter 6 is most relevant from the point of view of the Centre and the states as it goes into normative aspect of justness of actual transfers.

TABLE 5.3 : **The results of desired transfer from the centre to various states**

(Stage Three)

(Rs. lakhs)

States	1957-58		1961-62		1964-65		1967-68		1976-77	
	Desired	Actual	Desired	Actual	Desired	Actual	Desired	Actual	Desired	Actual
1. Andhra Pradesh	898	1407	1586	1975	1038	3080	5060	4657	8461	25125
2. Assam	151	775	468	965	848	1466	1778	2883	5041	14749
3. Bihar	1803	1589	1538	2130	857	2620	—	—	28542	18452
4. Gujarat	—	—	844	1869	149	2138	2165	2386	3659	8299
5. Jammu & Kashmir	141	445	110	498	962	529	1359	1295	760	8663
6. Karnataka	664	1241	846	1557	1217	2045	1758	4320	8810	10868
7. Kerala	1515	611	1080	825	847	1717	743	3736	9771	11527
8. Madhya Pradesh	243	1121	425	1569	567	2184	4225	3188	16707	19372
9. Maharashtra	2908	1938	2110	1582	1959	3070	2018	5202	1392	23814
10. Orissa	425	787	2513	1024	1782	2528	3733	4605	7662	8610
11. Punjab	332	779	1243	1144	760	1483	—	—	—	5649
12. Rajasthan	117	764	944	1045	1893	1764	4437	2573	11563	13934
13. Tamil Nadu	623	990	1318	1563	1698	2326	4590	4137	12265	12503
14. Uttar Pradesh	1716	1975	3784	3172	3653	3747	8578	7362	33141	27208
15. West Bengal	3441	1590	2254	2174	2268	2414	4232	4600	4942	15123
16. Haryana									830	
17. Himachal Pradesh									—	
18. Meghalaya									—	
19. Tripura									—	

TABLE 5.4 : **The results of desired transfer from the centre to various states (Three Stages)**

(*Rs. lakhs*)

States	1957-58 (1)	1957-58 (2)	1957-58 (3)	1961-62 (1)	1961-62 (2)	1961-62 (3)	1964-65 (1)	1964-65 (2)	1964-65 (3)	1967-68 (1)	1967-68 (2)	1967-68 (3)	1976-77 (1)	1976-77 (2)	1976-77 (3)
1. Andhra Pradesh	1457	806	898	2978	1434	1586	2547	984	1038	6372	4729	5060	23381	8378	8461
2. Assam	–435	136	151	191	432	468	529	799	848	667	1669	1778	11422	4814	5041
3. Bihar	5289	1374	1803	8125	1461	1538	11110	791	857	—	—	—	55060	26423	28542
4. Gujarat	—	—	—	–207	779	844	–180	139	149	965	2016	2165	–18195	3388	3659
5. Jammu & Kashmir	175	153	141	–106	106	110	153	951	962	24	1321	1358	1004	637	760
6. Karnataka	143	570	664	630	796	846	1260	1154	1217	2857	1652	1758	9040	8715	8810
7. Kerala	983	1053	1515	1385	1007	1080	1256	771	847	2524	692	743	7071	9302	9771
8. Madhya Pradesh	1660	332	243	2496	386	425	2562	523	567	8095	3986	4225	35200	16611	16707
9. Maharashtra	–771	2459	2908	–3623	2045	2110	–7253	1864	1959	–4975	1877	2018	–74405	1309	1392
10. Orissa	1709	580	426	2020	2428	2513	2657	1782	1782	4412	3500	3733	17178	7119	7662
11. Punjab	–1943	306	332	–2597	1173	1243	–7707	689	760	–10055	–275	—	–47985	–3888	—
12. Rajasthan	554	144	117	1045	873	944	2160	1728	1893	4368	4204	4437	14505	11107	11563
13. Tamil Nadu	525	651	623	274	1224	1318	689	1630	1698	1081	4312	4590	21899	11688	12265
14. Uttar Pradesh	3662	1702	1716	9845	3554	3784	9892	3191	3653	20792	8003	8578	67581	30590	33141
15. West Bengal	–123	2442	3411	1205	2134	2254	2735	2178	2268	6129	3969	4232	14442	4922	4942
16. Haryana										–15771	749	830	–15771	749	830
17. Himachal Pradesh										–91	–1945		–91	–1945	—
18. Meghalaya										984	–2640		984	–2640	—
19. Tripura										1236	–3080		1236	–3080	—

6

A PROBABLE CRITERION FOR EVALUATING JUSTNESS OF ACTUAL TRANSFERS

A Case Study of Indian States

STATES have been complaining of growing imbalance between their requirements and resources. This complaint has been accentuated by the change in income tax, whereby the income tax paid by companies was brought in the category of corporate taxation, which is not a divisible item under the Constitution. Also, replacement of state sales tax by additional union excise duties in respect of a number of additional products has further reduced the elasticity of state tax resources. It may be noted that in assessing the complaint made by states, it is the total transfers, both for plan and non-plan expenditure, that should be taken into account. It is possible that inadequate transfers for non-plan expenditure may be more than compensated by transfers for plan expenditure. In this chapter we have computed the amount of desired transfer under five alternative approaches to evaluate the justness of actual transfers as per the recommendations of the various Finance Commissions. Justness being normative concept it has been defined in a probable manner. This exercise, therefore, provides a partial assessment of the problem of transfer of resources.

For analytical purposes, the complaint made by states may be divided into two parts : (*a*) inadequate allocation from the centre to the states ; and (*b*) improper distribution of the allocated resources among different states. The solution to the first part is provided by taking into account an alternative approach for allocation of resources based on the concepts of standard tax and standard revenue. The answer to the second part of the problem is provided by a comparison between actual transfers and desired transfers under alternative approaches. If, on the basis of comparison, some states are observed to have been discriminated against, then the distribution can be said to be improper and unjust. The layout of the paper is as follows : Section one is divided into four subsections. In subsection one, the alternative approaches considered are given. Subsection two gives the notation used and symbolic presentation of alternative approaches. Subsection three gives reasons for adopting the period of study ranging from 1957-58 to 1967-68. Subsection four states the assumptions underlying this study. Section two discusses a probable definition of the concept of justness. Section three has been subdivided into four parts. Subsection one analyses the results of desired transfer as per the fourth approach with actual transfers. Subsection two compares actual transfer with the desired transfer under all alternative approaches. Subsection three compares actual transfers with the desired transfers under the second approach and that under the fifth. Subsection four analyses the results of desired transfer under the third approach with those under the second. Section four concludes by giving a summary of findings.

SECTION I

Alternative approaches

The first approach suggests allocation of resources exclusively on the basis of tax effort of states. The tax effort stands for the ratio of state tax revenue to the income of the given state. This approach assumes that the capacity of a state to raise tax is dependent on its income regardless of the number of persons in the State. This assumption is not very correct because the taxable capacity is dependent on the per capita income rather than the total income. For instance, consider a hypothetical situation where two states S_1 and S_2 have identical income Y, but the population of the first state is twice that of the second state. In this case it shall not be correct to expect that both the states should raise the same amount of tax to have identical tax effort. The effect of implementing this approach shall be to inflate the desired transfer to states with the same amount of income but with lesser population.

The second approach tries to correct the defect of the first approach by redefining tax effort as the ratio of state taxes to the per capita income of the given state. It may be noted that this approach is very similar to the Nixon Administration Proposal for allocation of grants.[1] But there is a minor difference. In the case of Nixon Administration Proposal the allocation is based on the comparative revenue effort, while our approach suggests allocation on the basis of comparative tax effort of states. The reason for preferring tax effort over revenue effort lies in the fact that setting up a plant in the state for producing some public good may be dependent on climatic factors over which a state may not have any control. The impact of this approach shall be to reward states with per capita tax effort above average. This may encourage states to raise a higher percentage of their per capita income as tax. If extra resources so made available are used for further investment, the implementation of this scheme shall augment the rate of economic growth.

The third approach introduces an additional variable to the second to assign weightage to consistency in the tax efforts of States. This approach is very similar to the one given by the Advisory Commission on Inter-governmental Relationship in the U.S.A.[2] The only difference lies in substituting tax effort for revenue effort for the reason mentioned in the preceding paragraph. A comparison of results based on this approoch with those based on the second shall be able to throw light on the consistency in the tax effort of the states. This part of the exercise has some economic significance. If the states with per capita income above the average are as inconsistent in their tax effort as the states with per capita income below the average, it may imply that states do not have any control over the tax they raise and that capacity to raise tax may be dependent upon economic conditions prevailing in the state. If economic conditions determine the tax effort, it increases the responsibility of the central government to minimise fluctuations in the economic activity through various corrective measures. If, on the other hand, states are constrained by the tax effort of the neighbouring states in particular and other states in general, it may call for uniformity in prescribing the tax rate to have additional resources for rapid rate of economic growth. For instance, leaving the discretion with states for implementing a particular tax may dissuade a state to take an unpleasant decision.

The fourth approach[3] suggests allocation of resources on the basis of the difference between standard expenditure and standard revenue where standard expenditure and standard revenue are notional concepts indicating the amount of expenditure that shall be incurred and the revenue that shall be raised if the average of conditions prevailing in all states were to be applied in the case of individual states. For computing standard expenditure different heads of expenditure have been divided into three categories. The first category consists of those heads on which standard expenditure has been calculated on the basis of individual appropriate yardsticks and includes expenditure on education, medical and public health, irrigation, agriculture, industry, community development and public debts. The second category comprises of those items on which standard expenditure has been computed on the same basis, that is, percentage of total revenue expenditure on the given head and includes expenditure on tax collection, police and law and order, general administration, printing and stationery, pensions and forests. The third category includes those items on which actual expenditure incurred has been taken as standard because of unpredictable nature of items. The other determinant of desired transfer is the sum of standard tax revenue and standard non tax revenue. Standard tax revenue is calculated by computing the ratio of state tax revenue to income of all states and multiplying this ratio by the income of the given state. Standard non-tax revenue, likewise, has been calculated by computing the ratio of non-tax revenue to revenue receipts for all states and multiplying this ratio by the actual revenue receipts of given state. Since the desired transfer is given by the difference between the standard expenditure and standard revenue, the sum of desired transfer for all states represents an approximate measure of budgetary gap for all states. Therefore, if the sum of desired transfer for all states is less than the sum of actual transfers, it slightly weakens the force of the complaint that transfer of resources from the centre had been inadequate. This, however, may not be a proper way for judging the adequacy of transfers, for standard expenditure has been calculated on the basis of average of actual expenditure which may be unusually low because of lack of funds with states. To this it may be argued that state tax revenue may also be at a depressed figures. Thus, this approach shall provide a very crude way of assessing the adequacy of transfers from the centre to states. To throw light on the distribution of transfers among states, desired transfer to individual states should be corrected to be equal to the sum of actual transfers.

The fifth approach suggests allocation of resources exclusively on the basis of population. This approach obviously shall be favourable to states with population above the average. This approach assumes that requirements of states are primarily dependent on the number of persons. If poor states happen to be with population below the average, this approach shall not be able to remove regional imbalances in the level of economic development. It may be noted that there are a number of other approaches[4] but we have not included them in this exercise on account of certain flaws.

Notation used and symbolic presentation of different approaches

K : is the exogenously determined amount of the divisible pool (in this exercise it is the sum of actual transfers to all states as per the recommendations of various Finance Commissions) ;

G_i : is the amount of the divisible pool that should accrue to the 'i'-th state ;

ST_i : is the state tax revenue of the 'i'-th state ;
ST_i : is the summation of the state tax revenue for all states ;
Y_i : is the income of the 'i'-th state ;
Y_i : is the summation of income for all states ;
$ST_{i,\,t-1}$: is the state tax revenue of the 'i'-th state in the previous year ;
$Y_{i,\,t-1}$: is the previous year's income of the 'i'-th state ;
G^*_i : is the uncorrected desired transfer to the 'i'-th state under the fourth approach ;
P_i : is the population of the 'i'-th state ;
P_i : is the summation of the population of all states ;
E_i : is the standard expenditure of the 'i'-th state and is the sum of standard expenditure on three categories ;
R_i : is the standard revenue of the 'i'-th state and is the sum of standard tax revenue and standard non-tax revenue.

Approach I : $$G_i = \frac{\dfrac{ST_i}{Y_i}}{\sum_{i=1}^{n}\left(\dfrac{ST_i}{Y_i}\right)} \times K$$

Approach II : $$G_i = \frac{\left(\dfrac{ST_i}{Y_i \times P_i}\right)}{\sum_{i=1}^{n}\left(\dfrac{ST_i}{Y_i \times P_i}\right)} \times K$$

Approach III : $$G_i = \frac{\left(\dfrac{ST_i}{Y_i \times P_i}\right)\left\{\left(\dfrac{ST_i}{Y_i}\right) \div \left(\dfrac{ST_{i,\,t-1}}{Y_{i,\,t-1}}\right)\right\}}{\sum_{i=1}^{n}\left(\dfrac{ST_i}{Y_i \times P_i}\right)\left\{\left(\dfrac{ST_i}{Y_i}\right) \div \left(\dfrac{ST_{i,\,t-1}}{Y_{i,\,t-1}}\right)\right\}} \times K$$

Approach IV : $G_i^* = E_i - R_i$ and $$G_i = \left(\frac{G_i^*}{\sum_{i=1}^{n} G_i^*}\right) \times K$$

Approach V : $G_i = \left(\frac{P_i}{\sum_{i=1}^{n} P_i} \right) \times K$

Period of study

The period of study ranges from 1957-58 to 1967-68. The year 1957-58 is the financial year immediately following that of states' reorganisation. This has kept away the problems arising out of states' reorganisation. The year 1967-68 was the last year for which information relating to various variables was available. It is hoped that a period of eleven years and five different approaches shall be able to evaluate the problem with a reasonable amount of accuracy. Despite delimiting the period of study to eleven years, bifurcation of Bombay took place during the period of study. The same was true for Punjab. Also a new state was formed in between the period of study. This raised certain problems. As a consequence, information relating to Bombay before its bifurcation has been shown against Maharashtra, while after the bifurcation of Punjab state, information shown relates to newly constituted state of Punjab. The difficulty regarding obtaining information on Haryana and Nagaland dissuaded us in including these states in the exercise.

Assumptions

This study is based on the following simplifying assumptions : First, that the amount of divisible pool shall be able to meet unfulfilled requirements of states. The states may have reservations about this assumption but to be strictly comparable, the sum of actual transfers has been taken as the amount of divisible pool.

Second, the tax effort of a state is attributed to the deliberate measures taken by its state government and is assumed to be devoid of differences on account of natural and climatic factors. This assumption is not a very realistic one but making adjustments for differences relating to various factors requires information on a number of variables which is not available.

Also, an indirect measure of the differences prevailing in states is provided by differences in their income.

Third, a state with tax effort above the average, thus being entitled to a proportionately higher amount, is assumed to utilize funds, so made available, for enhancing rate of economic growth. The violation of this assumption shall amount to subsidizing unproductive expenditure of such states.

Fourth, the population of a state represents a good index of its requirements. There may be little dispute about this assump ion because expenditure on education, medical and public health and a host of other items depends upon the number of persons. The only drawback about this assumption is that it seems to identify poor states with those with population above the average. This is not true for some poor states, and to that extent, this approach may not be able to remove disparities prevailing in different regions.

Fifth, if states do not suffer from being discriminated against both in the absolute sense and the relative sense, as defined in section two, the procedure for allocation of resources is considered to be just. This is the most crucial assumption and a non-acceptance of this assumption shall modify the results.

Sixth, all states classified as those with per capita tax effort above the average are homogeneous. Similarly, states with per capita tax effort below the average are assumed to be almost similar in all relevant respects. This assumption shall preclude minor differences among states making the results inapplicable.

SECTION II

Justness may be defined as a situation in which states are not being discriminated against both in the absolute and the relative sense. *A priori*, second approach shall be favourable to states with per capita tax effort above the average and shall endeavour to enhance rate of economic growth by making additional resources available through state taxation. The fifth approach, on the other hand, shall distribute resources on the basis of population thereby removing regional disparities in different regions. Given these as the objective function of the decision making body, no state should receive an amount less than the desired transfer under the second approach and the fifth approach.

A state with tax effort above the average shall be said to be discriminated against in the absolute sense if it receives an amount less than the desired transfer under the fifth approach. It shall be construed to have been discriminated against in the relative sense if some state (states) with per capita tax effort below the average receives an amount higher than the desired transfer under the fifth approach.

A state with tax effort below the average shall be said to be discriminated against in the absolute sense if it received an amount less than the desired transfer under the second approach. It shall be construed to have been discriminated against in the relative sense if some state with per capita tax effort above the average receives an amount more than the desired transfer under the second approach.

From the propositions given above, it follows that the procedure for allocation of resources among states shall be just if no state receives an amount beyond the range of desired transfer based on the second approach and the fifth.

To accommodate minor differences in the states classified as states with per capita tax effort above the average and below the average, the actual transfers have been compared with results of desired transfer under all alternative approaches. (See Section III).

It may be observed that the desired transfer under any approach that shall combine the objective function of encouraging tax effort with that of removal of regional disparities in the level of economic development, shall be within the range of zone of justness. The results of cases of unjustness, stated earlier, as per the definition of justness given above, shall still be applicable though there may be additions to the cases of unjustness on account of narrowing of the range within which transfers are said to be just.

SECTION III

Analysis of allocation of resources between the centre and the states

A perusal of total uncorrected desired transfer under the fourth approach and the divisible pool indicates that states received an amount higher than the desired transfer at each point of time. See Tables 6.1 to 6.12 given at the end of the chapter. Though a crude procedure for evaluating the transfer from the centre to states, the results suggest that the total transfers have not been inadequate to meet the budgetary gap. But the actual expenditure of the states may have been at an unduly depressed level on account of non-availability of funds. A correction for this presupposes that information on average expenditure, considered desirable on various heads, is available. In the absence of information on this aspect, this extension was not carried out in this exercise. However, since the gap between the actual transfers and the desired transfers is fairly wide, there may not have been change in the ultimate outcome.

Analysis of actual transfers with desired transfers under the alternative approaches

In this and the following subsection, we attempt an evaluation of the justness or otherwise of the actual transfers. The analysis of this subsection is based on a broader interpretation of justness. According to this interpretation, actual transfer to any state shall be construed to be just if it is within the range of desired transfers given by the five alternative approaches. A perusal of tables one to eleven shows that states may be divided into four categories. The first category consists of those states which received funds more than the desired transfer in certain years without receiving less than the desired transfer at any point of time. The second category consists of those states which received an amount within the range determined by the desired transfer under alternative approaches. The third category consists of those states for which results are not uniform over the entire period of study.

These states received more than the desired transfer in certain years while the opposite was true at other points of time. The fourth category consists of those states which received an amount less than the desired transfer under all alternative approaches in certain years without receiving more in any year.

Andhra Pradesh, Assam, Mysore and Orissa belong to the first category. These states received more than desired transfer at two, three, four and five points of time respectively. This phenomenon is the result of high magnitude of actual transfers on account of transfers under statutory grants. For instance, the revenue deficit as worked out by the Fourth Finance Commission for the five year period was the highest for Orissa (Rs. 145.90 crores); the third highest for Mysore (Rs. 91.20 crores); the fourth highest for Assam (Rs. 82.60 crores); and Rs. 36.10 crores for Andhra Pradesh. One-fifth of this has accrued to these states as the annual grant. The actual transfer to Andhra Pradesh has been of a high order because of a higher percentage of share out of the divisible pool which has been mostly allocated on the basis of population. From the above it follows that these states have very little reason to complain against the distribution of divisible resources among states.

Bihar, Jammu & Kashmir and Uttar Pradesh belong to the second category. These states have not been discriminated against at least in the absolute sense as the actual transfer to these states is always within the range determined by the desired transfers. Jammu & Kashmir belongs to this category because of the desired transfer under the first approach which is of a very high magnitude for this state. As will be seen in the analysis of the following subsection of Jammu & Kashmir belongs to that category of states which received more than the desired transfer at all points of time. Madhya Pradesh belongs to this group primarily because of high magnitude of non-plan-non-statutory grants. For instance, it received the highest amount under this head from 1961-62 to 1965-66 which was of the order of Rs. 1120 lakhs, Rs. 1056 lakhs, Rs. 1061 lakhs, Rs. 1685 lakhs and Rs. 1698 lakhs respectively. This has been responsible for inflating the actual transfers thereby making these compare favourably with the desired transfers. The states belonging to this category can only complain of having been discriminated against in the relative sense.

Gujarat and West Bengal belong to the third category. Gujarat received more at one point of time while it received less than the desired transfer during the last two points of observations. It received more in 1960-61, the year in which this state was formed, and included a substantial amount under non-plan-non-statutory grant. During the last two years, the actual transfer has been less than the desired because of its having a budgetary surplus and hence not being entitled to any amount under Article 275. The actual transfer to West Bengal was more at one point of time but it received less than the desired transfer at five points of observation. Therefore, its position is nearer to the states belonging to the second category. From 1962-63 to 1966-67 the actual transfer has been less than the desired because it did not receive any significant amount as grant-in-aid. This is because it has been ascertained to be a state with a surplus budget as per the calculations of the Finance Commission. From the above, it follows that these states may complain of having been discriminated against in the relative sense.

Kerala, Madras, Maharashtra, Punjab and Rajasthan belong to the fourth category and have been discriminated against in the absolute sense. These states received less than the desired transfer at three, four, two, one and one point (points) of time respectively. The only redeeming feature is that this situation is no more continuing as can be seen from the results relating to concluding points of observations. For instance, Kerala never received less than the desired transfer from 1962-63 onwards. The magnitude of actual transfers has increased substantially because of huge transfers as statutory grants. According to the Fourth Finance Commission, the budgetary gap in its case turned out to be second highest, that is, Rs. 93.40 which was to accrue to it in five equal instalments. Since the states of Madras, Maharashtra and Punjab have per capita income above the average, their complaint of being discriminated against is as such not a very serious cause of concern. Further, Punjab received less than the desired transfer only during 1962-63 while Maharashtra during 1957-58 and 1961-62. Similarly, Rajasthan received less than the desired transfer only during 1967-68. These situations are like exceptional cases and an outcome of sudden changes in economic conditions while the recommendations about the actual transfers are made once in five years. Madras has been discriminated against consistently from 1962-63 to 1965-66. But the desired transfer according to the first approach in 1962-63 is Rs. 2098 lakhs compared to Rs. 2071 lakhs of actual transfer. Similarly, the difference is not substantial for 1963-64. The difference between the desired and the actual transfers is fairly wide for 1964-65 and 1965-66. But the corrective action seems to have started and for the concluding points of observation, the actual transfer is within the zone of just transfers.

Analysis of actual transfers and the desired transfers based on the second and the fifth approach

The results of this subsection are based on the strict interpretation of justness. As a result, the findings are more assertive because some states received more than the desired transfer at each point of time while others received less at most points of observation. A scrutiny of tables one to eleven shall indicate that states may be divided into three categories. The first category consists of those states which received more than the desired transfer at each point of time and includes Assam, Jammu & Kashmir, Mysore and Orissa. Andhra Pradesh may also be included in this category for it received more at seven points of time without receiving less than the desired transfer on any point of observation. There is no second category similar to the one of the previous subsection because no state received within the desired transfer under the second and the fifth approach at each point of time. Therefore the second category of this subsection consists of those states for which results are not uniform and includes Gujarat, Kerala, Punjab, Rajasthan and West Bengal. The third category consists of those states which received less than the desired transfer on most occasions (with the exceptions of Madhya Pradesh) without receiving more than the desired transfer at any point of time and includes Bihar, Madhya Pradesh, Madras, Maharashtra and Uttar Pradesh.

The first category of states has definitely not been discriminated against both in the absolute and the relative sense. The new entrant to this category, compared to that of the previous subsection, is Jammu & Kashmir. This is because of not taking into account the desired transfer under the first approach. For other states as well the results are more pronounced. Assam and Jammu & Kashmir received more than the desired transfer at each point of time because their population is below average, while their tax effort which is above average (under the first approach) turns out to be below the average in per capita terms. The desired transfer under the first approach, which has not been taken into account, is almost double of that under any other approach for these two states. The other states like Mysore, Orissa and Andhra Pradesh belong to this category because of heavy transfers as grants-in-aid.

In the second category, Gujarat received more at five points of time but less than the desired transfer during the last two points of time. Thus its position is similar to the states belonging to the first category. The actual transfers, during the last two points of time, are less than the desired transfers because it has been observed to be a state with surplus budget and hence not entitled to any amount under Article 275. For Kerala, the results are fair on the whole. It received less than the desired transfer during the first five points of time but more during the last six points of observation. Punjab, a state with per capita income above the average, received more at four points of time, less during the last three years and within the desired transfers during the other points of observation. This situation is an outcome of its being a state with both tax effort and the population below the average. Actual transfers during the last three points of time are less than the desired because it is a state with surplus budget. Rajasthan received more at five points of time while received less than the desired transfer during the last two years. This state seems to be having adequate funds for budgetary purposes and, therefore, has received very little as grants-in-aid. West Bengal received more at two points of time but less than the desired transfers during the last six years. The magnitude of actual transfers is low because of negligible amount as grants-in-aid for meeting the budgetary gap. For instance, it received a nominal statutory grant of Rs. 79 lakhs from 1962-63 to 1965-66 while it has been declared to be a state with surplus budget by the Fourth Finance Commission.

The states in the third category have been discriminated against both in the absolute and the relative sense. This category includes primarily those states which have both per capita tax effort and population above the average. This is true for Bihar, Madras, Maharashtra and Uttar Pradesh. The calculations of the Fourth Finance Commission indicate that Bihar, Maharashtra and Uttar Pradesh are states with surplus budgets and hence no statutory grant has been assigned to these states. Despite substantial transfers as non-plan-non-statutory grants, the transfers to Madhya Pradesh have been less than the desired transfers. This pattern of distribution of funds to states belonging to this category does not appear to be coincidental. For instance, Bihar received less than the desired transfers on seven out of nine points of time; Madras on ten out of eleven; Maharashtra and Uttar Pradesh on nine out of eleven; and Madhya Pradesh on three out of eleven. Heavy transfers as non-plan-non-statutory grants have been able to restrict the phenomenon of actual transfers being less than the desired to three points of time. The states in this category have a genuine reason for complaining of improper distribution of the divisible resources.

A note on the consistency of tax efforts of different states

A comparison of desired transfer under the third approach with that under the second shall indicate that the states for which the desired transfer under the third approach is more than that under the second on more than five points of observation are Assam, Gujarat, Jammu & Kashmir, Kerala and Orissa. Out of these Gujarat is the only state with per capita income above the average. The other prosperous states like Maharasthra, Punjab and West Bengal have been inconsistent on larger occasions than consistent. This indicates that even the prosperous states do not have sufficient control on their tax effort or have not exercised the same.

SECTION IV

Summary of findings

This chapter has attempted to evaluate the justness of actual transfers on the basis of a particular criterion of justness. Total transfers to states appear to have been reasonable if meeting the budgetary gap is the objective function of actual transfers. But this finding is subject to a qualifying condition that expenditure actually incurred by the states was not unduly low for lack of funds with the states. This is quite an improbable condition and hence the validity of these results is subject to the correctness of this condition. The second aspect of the problem related to the distribution of transfers among states. Here, Assam, Jammu & Kashmir, Mysore and Orissa appear to have received more than the desired transfer at all points of time and Andhra Pradesh received more on most of the points of observation. These states, therefore, have not been discriminated against both in the absolute and the relative sense. Bihar, Madras, Maharashtra and Uttar Pradesh received less than the desired transfer on most points of observation, without receiving more at any point of time. The same was true for West Bengal except that besides receiving less on most of the occasions it received more than the desired transfer on two occasions. These states, therefore, have been discriminated against both in the absolute and the relative sense. For the remaining states the results are not uniform. From the above it follows that the distribution of actual transfers has not been just. Another significant finding of this exercise is that most of the states have been inconsistent in their tax effort and that some of the richer states have been more inconsistent than consistent in their tax effort. In appendix to this chapter we present an analysis of results relating to 1976-77 to assess if there is any change in the composition of states.

Notes and References

1 The 1970 Nixon Administration Proposal, S. 2948, 91st Congress, 1st Session (1969).
2 Advisory Commission on Intergovernmental Relations, S. 2948, 91st Congress, 1st Session (1969).
3 O.P Chopra, "An Alternative Approach for Allocation of the Divisible Resources—A Case Study of Indian Stages", Conference Volume of the Indian Economic Association, December 1972, pp. 9-25.
4 We have not computed the desired transfers as per Zaveri's approach or that based on the scheme recommended by the Study Team on Centre-State Relationship because the weightage attached to various variables like population, per capita income, presence of people belonging to Scheduled Caste and so on, has been arbitrary. N.J. Zaveri, Transfer of non-plan resources to states, *Economic and Political Weekly*, Vol. IV, No. 23, (June 7, 1966), pp. 939-43. Government of India, Report of the Study Team on the Centre-State Relationship (June 1969).

TABLE 6.1 : **Results of desired transfer under alternative approaches from the centre to states for the year 1957-58**

(*Rs. Lakhs*)

States	First App.	Second App.	Third App.	Fourth App.	Fifth App.	Actual Transfer	Fourth* App.
Andhra Pradesh	1222	1338	1338	1016	1361	1407	807
Assam	1341	456	456	171	423	775	136
Bihar	929	1295	1295	1732	1733	1589	1375
Gujarat	—	—	—	—	—	—	—
Jammu & Kashmir	463	51	51	193	137	445	153
Kerala	1549	773	773	1326	621	611	1053
Madhya Pradesh	983	941	941	418	1190	1121	332
Madras	1193	1240	1240	820	1292	990	651
Maharashtra	2175	3867	3867	3096	2210	1938	2458
Mysore	1011	712	712	718	875	1241	570
Orissa	694	365	365	731	655	787	580
Punjab	1024	612	612	386	743	779	306
Rajasthan	980	580	580	181	737	764	144
Uttar Pradesh	1072	2399	2399	2144	2781	1975	1702
West Bengal	1374	1382	1382	3077	1250	1590	2442
Total						16012	12709

*Uncorrected for its being equal to actual transfer.

TABLE 6.2 : **Results of desired transfer under alternative approaches from the centre to states for the year 1958-59**

(Rs. Lakhs)

States	First App.	Second App.	Third App.	Fourth App.	Fifth App.	Actual Transfer	Fourth App.
Andhra Pradesh	1522	1707	1706	1714	1714	1728	1177
Assam	1845	653	720	134	540	887	92
Bihar	1404	2014	2443	2213	2189	1836	1520
Gujarat	—	—	—	—	—	—	—
Jammu & Kashmir	735	83	106	246	172	496	169
Kerala	2062	1062	1135	1293	787	723	888
Madhya Pradesh	977	965	770	Neg.	1509	1366	Neg.
Madras	1260	1337	1132	974	1621	1320	669
Maharashtra	2489	4567	4192	4562	2802	2925	3133
Mysore	1526	1105	1338	439	1107	1402	302
Orissa	845	457	446	866	827	903	593
Punjab	1258	777	765	932	943	1014	643
Rajasthan	1174	719	691	450	935	920	309
Uttar Pradesh	1207	2769	2500	2692	3503	2690	1849
West Bengal	1942	2028	2300	3657	1595	1936	2512
Total						20176	13856

TABLE 6.3 : **Results of desired transfer under alternative approaches from the centre to states for the year 1959-60**

(Rs. Lakhs)

States	First App.	Second App.	Third App.	Fourth App.	Fifth App.	Actual Transfer	Fourth App.
Andhra Pradesh	1710	1849	1907	1419	1780	1825	1115
Assam	1204	417	250	294	570	916	231
Bihar	1543	2138	2155	1717	2282	1912	1350
Gujarat	—	—	—	—	—	—	—
Jammu & Kashmir	803	87	87	298	178	506	234
Kerala	1878	934	777	1058	824	762	832
Madhya Pradesh	1248	1196	1402	32	1579	1446	25
Madras	1584	1614	1862	1094	1677	1412	860
Maharashtra	2564	4568	4318	5611	2932	3044	4412
Mysore	1601	1123	1081	719	1155	1455	565
Orissa	866	453	427	963	862	942	757
Punjab	1333	799	777	934	988	1057	734
Rajasthan	1403	835	915	670	980	972	527
Uttar Pradesh	1379	3049	3196	3313	3641	2876	2605
West Bengal	2022	2064	1972	2909	1680	2003	2287
Total						21028	16534

TABLE 6.4 : **Results of desired transfer under alternative approaches from the centre to states for the year 1960-61**

(*Rs. Lakhs*)

States	First App.	Second App.	Third App.	Fourth App.	Fifth App.	Actual Transfer	Fourth App.
Andhra Pradesh	1955	2379	2489	2471	2056	2070	1561
Assam	1649	652	816	1002	668	993	633
Bihar	1611	2522	2410	1664	2646	2065	1015
Gujarat	1455	1006	968	1010	1168	1710	638
Jammu & Kashmir	965	117	128	361	205	512	228
Kerala	2118	1201	1247	1295	959	870	818
Madhya Pradesh	1300	1413	1347	287	1837	1652	181
Madras	1754	2004	2032	1050	1932	2003	663
Maharashtra	2000	2657	2131	2028	2245	1496	1281
Mysore	1723	1368	1347	814	1341	1691	514
Orissa	968	572	585	1569	999	1069	991
Punjab	1906	1297	1698	1762	1:51	1198	1113
Rajasthan	1404	949	869	1091	1142	1110	689
Uttar Pradesh	1550	3862	3976	4-48	4211	3456	2683
West Bengal	2170	2527	2482	3876	1968	2633	2448
Total						24528	15456

TABLE 6.5 : **Results of desired transfer under alternative approaches from the centre to states for the year 1961-62**

(*Rs. Lakhs*)

States	First App.	Second App.	Third App.	Fourth App.	Fifth App.	Actual Transfer	Fourth App.
Andhra Pradesh	1601	2014	1745	1669	1934	1975	1435
Assam	1621	673	700	503	638	965	432
Bihar	1424	2314	2165	1701	2496	2130	1461
Gujarat	2533	1827	3365	907	1108	1869	779
Jammu & Kashmir	890	111	108	123	191	498	106
Kerala	1964	1160	1138	1172	908	825	1009
Madhya Pradesh	1224	1385	1380	449	1740	1569	386
Madras	1513	1782	1627	1425	1810	1563	1224
Maharashtra	1708	2362	2135	2381	2126	1582	2045
Mysore	1600	1319	1296	927	1268	1557	796
Orissa	982	603	647	2827	943	1024	2428
Punjab	1588	1039	916	1366	1006	1144	1173
Rajasthan	1321	931	927	1014	1083	1045	873
Uttar Pradesh	1296	3342	2957	4138	3692	3172	3555
West Bengal	1826	2230	1985	2485	1877	2174	2134
Total						23092	19836

TABLE 6.6 : **Results of desired transfer under alternative approaches from the centre to states for the year 1962-63**

(*Rs. Lakhs*)

States	First App.	Second App.	Third App.	Fourth App.	Fifth App.	Actual Transfer	Fourth App.
Andhra Pradesh	2150	2646	2686	2147	2481	2810	1632
Assam	1936	794	716	546	826	1363	415
Bihar	1969	3140	3280	1987	3214	2286	1510
Gujarat	2308	1641	1130	305	1434	1966	232
Jammu & Kashmir	1211	147	151	813	244	528	618
Kerala	2424	1410	1316	1628	1172	1578	1237
Madhya Pradesh	1622	1809	1809	1012	2243	1953	769
Madras	2098	2411	2527	2211	2317	2071	1681
Maharashtra	2173	2959	2845	2803	2744	2676	2130
Mysore	2170	1757	1801	1875	1632	1868	1425
Orissa	1368	823	866	2674	1213	2384	2032
Punjab	2213	1434	1510	1729	1306	1315	1314
Rajasthan	1857	1292	1372	915	1403	1611	695
Uttar Pradesh	1786	4520	4706	5444	5101	3290	4137
West Bengal	2470	2974	3041	3667	2426	2058	2787
Total						29757	22614

TABLE 6.7 : **Results of desired transfer under alternative approaches from the centre to states for the year 1963-64**

(*Rs. Lakhs*)

States	First App.	Second App.	Third App.	Fourth App.	Fifth App.	Actual Transfer	Fourth App.
Andhra Pradesh	2483	3153	3291	2124	2817	3096	1277
Assam	2075	887	859	878	948	1484	528
Bihar	2036	3362	3142	2041	3663	2532	1227
Gujarat	2488	1840	1794	1138	1641	2164	684
Jammu & Kashmir	1558	194	225	1301	276	555	782
Kerala	2789	1683	1750	2070	1338	1742	1244
Madhya Pradesh	1698	1960	1855	469	2563	2213	282
Madras	2405	2845	2949	2720	2625	2331	1635
Maharashtra	2617	3700	4028	1068	3136	3013	642
Mysore	2407	1200	1203	1872	1107	2065	1125
Orissa	1570	978	1015	3059	1382	2561	1839
Punjab	2269	1534	1423	2193	1500	1503	1318
Rajasthan	2189	1587	1692	2584	1608	1783	1553
Uttar Pradesh	1831	4794	4444	5908	5807	3766	3551
West Bengal	2771	3468	3516	3562	2777	2379	2141
Total						32987	19828

TABLE 6.8: **Results of desired transfer under alternative approaches from the centre to states for the year 1964-65**

(*Rs. Lakhs*)

States	First App.	Second App.	Third App.	Fourth App.	Fifth App.	Actual Transfer	Fourth App.
Andhra Pradesh	2302	2926	2794	1700	2716	3080	984
Assam	2042	882	893	1380	923	1466	799
Bihar	1816	3013	2769	1367	3545	7620	791
Gujarat	2584	1929	2064	240	1595	2138	138
Jammu & Kashmir	1751	217	251	1643	264	529	951
Kerala	2748	1669	1694	1332	1298	1717	771
Madhya Pradesh	1827	2124	2375	904	2485	2184	523
Madras	2574	3041	3352	2816	2525	2326	1630
Maharashtra	2382	3393	3180	3230	3043	3070	1864
Mysore	2285	1926	1884	1994	1801	2045	1154
Orissa	1780	1113	1299	3078	1336	2528	1782
Punjab	2365	1619	1738	1191	1463	1483	689
Rajasthan	2052	1503	1451	2985	1566	1764	1728
Uttar Pradesh	1465	3852	3174	5512	5616	3747	3191
West Bengal	2903	3666	3957	3762	2699	2414	2178
Total						33111	19173

TABLE 6.9 : **Results of desired transfer under alternative approaches from the centre to states for the year 1965-66**

(*Rs. Lakhs*)

States	First App.	Second App.	Third App.	Fourth App.	Fifth App.	Actual Transfer	Fourth App.
Andhra Pradesh	2324	2827	2621	3523	2806	3226	3090
Assam	1454	607	397	1364	962	1544	1196
Bihar	1737	2769	3433	1308	3676	2825	1147
Gujarat	3608	2598	3331	1038	1661	2250	910
Jammu & Kashmir	1713	202	182	1274	272	563	1117
Kerala	2958	1729	1710	816	1349	1808	716
Madhya Pradesh	2028	2270	2315	2323	2581	2331	2037
Madras	2709	3056	2955	2534	2602	2447	2222
Maharashtra	2750	4634	4913	3000	3887	3193	2631
Mysore	2459	1991	1968	2169	1868	2145	1902
Orissa	1826	1096	1033	3970	1384	2647	3482
Punjab	2332	1545	1400	Neg.	1528	1483	Neg.
Rajasthan	2185	1547	1513	2550	1632	1863	2236
Uttar Pradesh	1665	4201	4384	5227	5819	3992	4584
West Bengal	3092	3766	3684	3743	2809	2521	3283
Total						34838	30553

TABLE 6.10 : **Results of desired transfer under alternative approaches from the centre to states for the year 1966-67**

(*Rs. Lakhs*)

States	First App.	Second App.	Third App.	Fourth App.	Fifth App.	Actual Transfer	Fourth App.
Andhra Pradesh	3105	4046	3799	4978	4357	4169	4489
Assam	2755	1243	1656	1895	1508	2777	1709
Bihar	N.A.	N.A.	N.A.	N.A.	N.A.	N.A.	N.A.
Gujarat	5366	4175	4360	2429	2599	2180	2191
Jammu & Kashmir	2627	330	356	1502	419	1246	1355
Kerala	4371	2755	2862	1190	2108	3575	1073
Madhya Pradesh	2719	3269	3080	5647	4019	2824	5093
Madras	3483	4200	3796	5286	4031	3714	4767
Maharashtra	4311	6374	7022	2811	4943	4560	2535
Mysore	3573	3112	3178	2436	2911	4051	2197
Orissa	2341	1509	1360	3830	2155	4460	3454
Punjab	3370	2418	2444	71	2399	1395	64
Rajasthan	3103	2375	2371	5374	2559	2362	4847
Uttar Pradesh	2382	6457	6495	7819	9062	6772	7052
West Bengal	3960	5206	4686	5012	4395	3371	4520
Total						50281	45346

TABLE 6.11 : **Results of desired transfer under alternative approaches from the centre to states for the year 1967-68**

(Rs. Lakhs)

States	First App.	Second App.	Third App.	Fourth App.	Fifth App.	Actual Transfer	Fourth App.
Andhra Pradesh	3276	4330	4216	5727	4578	4657	4729
Assam	3717	1719	2140	2021	1601	2883	1669
Bihar	2271	3959	3505	N.A.	6040	N.A.	N.A.
Gujarat	5904	4687	4759	2442	2750	2386	2016
Jammu & Kashmir	3088	390	424	1600	438	1295	1321
Kerala	5015	3218	3408	838	2223	3736	692
Madhya Pradesh	3153	3871	4142	4828	4252	3188	3986
Madras	3736	4556	4509	5223	4222	4137	4312
Maharashtra	4597	6928	6819	2273	5219	5202	1877
Mysore	4136	3666	3917	2001	3069	4320	1652
Orissa	2603	1706	1750	4239	2270	4605	3500
Punjab	3241	1417	1258	333	1515	1133	Neg.
Rajasthan	3640	2849	3084	5091	2711	2573	4205
Uttar Pradesh	1971	5431	4146	9694	9543	7362	8003
West Bengal	4731	6351	7003	4807	4650	4600	3970
Total						52077	42207

TABLE 6.12 : **Desired transfer under alternative approaches from the centre to states in different years**

States	1957-58 I	1957-58 II	1957-58 III	1957-58 IV	1957-58 V	1957-58 VI	1961-62 I	1961-62 II	1961-62 III	1961-62 IV	1961-62 V	1964-65 I	1964-65 II	1964-65 III	1964-65 IV	1964-65 V
Andhra Pradesh	1122	1338	1338	1016	1361	1407	2150	2646	2686	2147	2481	2302	2926	2994	1700	2716
Assam	1341	456	456	171	423	755	1936	794	716	546	826	2042	882	893	1380	923
Bihar	929	1295	1295	1732	1733	1589	1969	3140	380	1987	3214	1816	3013	2769	1367	3545
Gujarat	—	—	—	—	—	—	2308	1641	1130	305	1434	2484	1929	2064	240	1595
J. & K.	463	51	51	193	137	445	1211	147	151	813	244	1751	217	251	1643	264
Karnataka	1011	712	712	718	875	1241	2170	1557	1801	1875	1632	2285	1926	1884	1994	1801
Kerala	1549	773	773	1326	621	611	2424	1410	1316	1628	1172	2748	1669	1694	1332	1298
Madhya Pradesh	983	941	941	418	1190	1121	1622	1800	1809	1012	2243	1827	2124	2375	904	2485
Maharashtra	2175	3867	3867	3096	2210	1938	2173	2959	2845	2803	2744	2382	3393	3180	3230	3043
Orissa	694	365	365	731	655	787	1368	823	866	2674	1213	1780	1113	1299	3078	1336
Punjab	1024	612	612	386	743	779	2213	1434	1510	1729	1306	2365	1619	1738	1191	1463
Rajasthan	980	580	580	181	737	764	1857	1292	1372	915	1403	2052	1503	1451	2985	1566
Tamil Nadu	1193	1240	1240	820	1292	990	2098	2411	2527	2211	2317	2594	3041	3352	2816	2525
U.P.	1072	2399	2399	2144	2781	1975	1786	4520	4706	5444	5101	1465	3852	3174	5512	5616
W. Bengal	1374	1382	1382	3077	1250	1590	2470	2974	3041	3667	2426	2903	3666	3957	3762	2699
Haryana																

(*Contd.*)

TABLE 6.12 (*Contd.*)

States	1967-68 I	II	III	IV	V	1976-77 I	II	III	IV	V	VI
Andhra Pradesh	3276	4330	4216	5727	4578	16457	24808		15380	19905	25125
Assam	3717	1719	2140	2021	1601	6898	3354		8837	7204	14749
Bihar	2271	3959	3505	—	6040	13229	23482		48508	25656	18452
Gujarat	5904	4687	4759	2442	2750	13895	11942		6219	12568	8299
J. & K.	3088	390	424	1600	438	13563	2012		1169	2125	8663
Karnataka	4136	3666	3917	2001	3069	16900	15699		15999	13473	10868
Kerala	5015	3218	3408	838	2223	19955	13552		17076	9944	11527
Madhya Pradesh	3153	3871	4142	4828	4252	14289	19457		30495	19586	19372
Maharashtra	4597	6928	6819	2273	5219	16728	26703		2403	23393	23814
Orissa	2603	1706	1750	4239	2270	9214	6306		13069	10127	8610
Punjab	3241	1417	1258	333	1515	17418	7514		7137	6207	1644
Rajasthan	3640	2849	3084	5091	2711	17270	14626		20390	12045	13934
Tamil Nadu	3736	4556	4509	5223	4222	17226	22872		21457	18863	12503
Uttar Pradesh	1971	5431	4146	9694	9543	12269	34083		56158	39931	27208
West Bengal	4731	6351	7003	4807	4650	12835	18115		9036	20674	15123
Haryana	—	—	—	—	—	14116	1696		1375	4659	6301

APPENDIX TO CHAPTER 6

A NOTE ON JUSTNESS OF ACTUAL TRANSFERS

In this note we present an analysis of justness of actual transfers updating the results to 1976-77, the latest year for which information on different indicators of normalisation was available. This exercise was not presented in the main part of the text because the results are not comparable in the strict sense. The reorganisation of the states took place. A number of new states have emerged. Since, we present the results in respect of the year 1976-77, the new names of the states have been used. This was not done earlier in the text of Chapter 6. We have new names such as Karnataka for the erstwhile state of Mysore and Tamil Nadu for Madras. We have presented the results in respect of Haryana. The results of Meghalaya, Tripura and Himachal Pradesh have not been presented because these are newly formed states and the allocation to these states is more than the desired transfer.

We may mention that unlike the results of the main text the sum of the desired transfer to all states exceeds the actual transfer. The actual transfer is Rs. 2301.92 crores as against the desired transfer of Rs. 2747.08 crores. Of course, these results are the stage two results and use individual yardsticks for normalisation.

In the following paragraphs we present the results of actual transfer and assess these against the desired allocation under the alternative approaches.

SECTION I

A comparison of results of desired transfer under alternative approaches with the actual transfer shows that states may be classified into four groups:

(1) States which received more than the desired transfer at some point in time without receiving less than the desired transfer at any point in time;

(2) States which received less than the desired transfer at

some points in time without receiving more than the desired transfer at any point in time;

(3) States which received an amount which fell within the range of desired transfer at all the points of study; and

(4) States for which the results are not uniform at some points in time they received more than the desired transfer and at other points the actual transfer fell short of the desired allocation.

States which received more than the desired transfer without receiving less than the desired transfer at any point in time

These states cannot complain that they have been discriminated against in the matter of transfer of resources on current account and include Andhra Pradesh, Assam and Orissa. The actual transfer exceeded the desired allocation under alternative approaches at four points in time in the case of Andhra Pradesh, two points in time in the case of Orissa and one point in the case of Assam. The first approach raises the amount of desired allocation to such a high level that the actual transfer falls within the range of desired transfer as given by the alternative approaches. This is particularly true for Assam, Jammu & Kashmir and Karnataka. But for the first approach the actual transfer to these states would have exceeded the desired allocation. Recall that the first approach recommends allocation on the basis of the relative tax effort of the States and is given by the ratio of proportion of tax effort to state's income of the given State to this proportion for all States. States which raise a higher proportion of their income as tax are rewarded by higher desired allocation relative to States with low proportion of tax effort to their income.

Andhra Pradesh received an allocation more than the desired transfer at four points in time. The only exception is the year 1967-68. Till the year 1978, this state was assessed to be a deficit state and was entitled to an allocation under Article 275. The position since then has changed and as per the Report of the Eighth Finance Commission this State is not a member of the States that have been identified as deficit states.

Obviously the actual allocation to this State shall register a fall.

Assam's actual transfer exceeds the desired allocation only during 1976-77. At other points of study the actual transfer falls within the range of desired allocation as given by alternative approaches. As mentioned earlier, the inclusion of first approach is responsible for actual transfer falling within the range of desired transfer.

Orissa received an amount more than the desired transfer at two points in time—1957-58 and 1967-68. At other points the actual allocation was within the range of desired allocation. Orissa continues to be identified as a deficit state and therefore the actual transfer may exceed the desired allocation. Recall that States are identified as deficit or surplus states after introducing corrections to forecasts of expenditure and revenue presented by the States. A fairly elaborate procedure is followed to work out the expenditure on irrigation schemes, civil constructions, revenues from public sector undertakings.

States which received less than the desired transfer at some point of study without receiving more than the desired allocation at any point

These States may be somewhat justified in complaining about the procedure to identify the quantum of actual transfer. This may be particularly true of Tamil Nadu and West Bengal. These States received less than the desired transfer at three points of observation. There is, therefore, a need to specify the reasons for such an outcome. The other states which belong to this group include (i) rich states—Gujarat, Maharashtra and Punjab and (ii) Rajasthan. However, all these States received an amount less than the desired allocation at one point in time and therefore it does not represent a very serious situation of being discriminated against. Recall that the first approach raises the level of desired allocation of the rich states to such an extent that the actual allocation falls within the range of transfers given by alternative approaches. But for this, the final outcome would have been very different.

The redeeming feature of the actual procedure followed for allocation of resources is that the difference between the desired allocation and the actual transfer is not of a very high magnitude in the case of West Bengal and Tamil Nadu though the actual transfers fell short of desired allocation at three points of study. Note that we have calculated the difference between the desired allocation under the fifth approach and the actual transfer because these states have per capita income above the average for the country. Therefore, these may be deemed to have been discriminated against, in the absolute sense, if the actual transfer fell short of desired allocation as given by fifth approach, which assigns highest priority to needy states.

The actual transfer to Tamil Nadu fell short of desired allocation by Rs. 9.64 crores and Rs. 2.00 crores during the period 1961-62 and 1964-65. However, the divergence between the desired and the actual allocation is of the order of Rs. 60 crores for the year 1976-77 which is quite disturbing.

The divergence between the desired allocation and the actual transfer is not of a very high order in the case of West Bengal though it occurred at three points of observation. For example, the actual transfer fell short of desired allocation by Rs. 3 crores during 1961-62, Rs. 5.20 crores during 1964-65 and Rs. 1.31 crores during 1967-68.

Except for Rajasthan, the other three states, which received less than the desired allocation, are the rich states. Actual transfer to Rajasthan gives a low value because of share of divisible taxes. Note that income tax and union excise duties are allocated predominantly on the basis of population and hence are relatively unfavourable to Rajasthan. However, the allocation under Article 275 provides a substantial amount. We may mention that for Rajasthan even this situation has changed as per the exercises carried out by the Eighth Finance Commission. Note that the actual transfer fell short of desired allocation by Rs. 2 crores only during 1967-68.

The rich states—Gujarat, Maharashtra and Punjab—received less than the desired transfer at one point of observation. The short-fall of the actual transfer from the desired allocation was of the order of Rs. 4 crores, Rs. 3 crores and Rs. 6 crores respectively. This, therefore, is not a very alarming situation.

States which received an allocation falling within the range of desired allocation as given by the alternative approaches

These states cannot argue that the actual transfer has been rather low. Depending upon the objectives of the disbursing authorities, the alternative approaches provide fairly wide range. It may be recalled that the procedure followed by different Finance Commissions combines the objective of providing resources to need-based states alongwith rewarding more efficient states.

The states with population above the average—Bihar, U.P. and Madhya Pradesh--fall in this group because the actual transfer is less than the desired allocation under approach five. If the exercise excludes approach five these states shall be observed to have received more than the desired transfer at most points of observation.

The states of Jammu & Kashmir, Kerala and Haryana belong to this group because of their tax effort as given by the proportion of taxes raised to their income. The high proportion of tax effort to income raises their desired allocation under first approach and this results in actual transfer falling within the range of desired allocations.

State for which the results are not uniform

Karnataka is the only state which belongs to this group. The actual transfer exceeds the desired allocation at two points of observation whereas the actual transfer is less than the desired allocation at one point in time.

It would be observed that the actual transfer is less than the desired by Rs. 26.05 crores in 1976-77. As against this the actual transfer exceeds the desired allocation by Rs. 1.84 crores in 1967-68 and Rs. 2.30 crores in 1957-58. Thus, if one takes into account the extent of divergence between the desired and the actual allocation the state belongs to group (*ii*) which received an allocation less than the desired transfer.

We do not propose to present an analysis of the results comparing actual transfers with desired allocation as given by approach two and approach five. The classification of the states may change considerably but this has not been attempted due to lack of strict comparability of results on account of formation of new states and reorganisation of the existing states. Similarly, the exercise incorporating consistency in the tax effort of the states in determining the desired allocation has not been attempted for want of strict comparability of results. It would be noticed that findings do not undergo a significant change due to the inclusion of results for the year 1976-77, relative to the findings presented in the text of Chapter 6.

7

SUMMARY OF FINDINGS AND FIELDS FOR FURTHER EXPLORATIONS

THE problem of allocation of resources has attracted the attention of a number of writers. Two extreme approaches to the allocation of funds from the Centre to the constituent States have been suggested by Scott and Buchanan as given in Chapter 2. Their recommendations have certain limitations regarding practical applicability. Scott's solution may not be acceptable due to the pressure of non-economic forces. Buchanan's contention may not be acceptable for its growth retarding effects within a certain time horizon. The technique suggested by us has attempted to provide a logical solution combining to some extent the objectives of these two approaches.

Our approach has a bias in favour of economically less developed States modified to some extent by altering the assumptions made for computing standard tax revenue. Even when an explicit weight is attached to efficiency only marginal changes occur in results. Realising the complex nature of the problem, we have calculated different sets of results. The acceptable set will be determined by the relative significance to be attached to balanced regional growth and maximisation of rate of growth.

One of the findings of this study is that Assam and Jammu & Kashmir have received an amount greater than what they deserved on economic considerations. Similarly Gujarat, Madras, Maharashtra, Mysore and Punjab deserved an amount lesser than the actual allocation. For other States the results are not uniform though Bihar and Uttar Pradesh deserved a greater allocation than the actuals in most of the years.

Apart from the above specific results, one of the merits of our approach has been standardisation of expenditure on different heads, given the validity of norms. No doubt, all the Finance Commissions[1] have also scrutinized the forecasts of expenditure as furnished by States to determine the magnitude of grants under Article 275. Our approach has a more definite statistical basis of standardizing expenditure as it is an *ex post* analysis.[2] It can, however, be of great use of in taking corrective measures in the future.

Another dimension of the study is that we have computed the standard tax revenue for each State and for the entire period of the study. This computation gives an approximate measure of the extent to which additional revenue could be raised through State taxation.[3]

The approach adopted by us computes desired transfer measured by the difference between standard expenditure and standard revenue. This is in contrast to the procedure followed by various Finance Commissions. According to their technique, each State is entitled to an amount representing its share in income tax, union excise duties, other divisible taxes and other types of compensations.[4] Thus our study provides an independent test of assessing the justness or otherwise of actual transfers according to the recommendations of various Finance Commissions.

In Chapter 4 the period of study has been extended up to 1980-81 to ascertain the amount of desired projected transfers under certain assumptions. These results, though of limited value, provide a rough measure of desired transfers under certain assumptions.

FIELDS FOR FURTHER EXPLORATIONS

(*a*) If relevant statistical information is available expenditure on different heads can be standardized on the basis of more appropriate characteristics.[5] For instance expenditure on medical and public health can be standardized on the basis of number of doctors. Expenditure on agriculture can be computed on the basis of number of persons employed in agriculture. For industry, capital employed in industry in various States can be adopted as the norm. In the case of community development, some indicator of economic backwardness of the State can be adopted as the basis. The difficulty in adopting these alternative norms relates to the absence of information for each State and for the entire period of study. Given the availability of statistical data on these alternative characteristics, one can ascertain the impact of changing the basis of standardisation on the magnitude of desired transfers.

(*b*) Standard expenditure and standard revenue can be adjusted to take account of the special needs and peculiar characteristics of the different States. Such an exercise may be a further field for exploration.

(*c*) As mentioned in Chapter 1, it is total transfer of funds from the Centre which is crucial from the point of view of States. This requires the adoption of some technique for the allocation of resources on capital account. Such a technique requires (*i*) data on determinants of marginal efficiency of capital, (*ii*) pattern of investment and so on. If estimation of allocation of funds made by this technique are added to the desired transfer of funds on current account a measure of total transfer of funds to each State will then be available.

Notes and References

1 Government of India, Reports of various Finance Commissions.

2 It is *ex post* because actual average cost on each head has to be known.

3 This level is indicated by the computed magnitude of standard tax raising capacity.

4 There was no other option because of the constitutional provisions.

5 See Government of India, Planning Commission (Programme Administration Division), *Data Relating to Indicators of Development—States.*

APPENDICES

APPENDIX I

PROVISIONS OF THE CONSTITUTION HAVING A BEARING ON THE WORK OF THE FINANCE COMMISSION

Article 246. Subject matter of laws made by Parliament and by the Legislature of States.

(1) Notwithstanding anything in clauses (2) and (3), Parliament has exclusive power to make laws with respect to any of the matters enumerated in List I in the Seventh Schedule (in this Constitution referred to as the "Union List").

(2) Notwithstanding anything in clause (3), Parliament, and subject to clause (1), the Legislature of any State also, have power to make laws with respect to any of the matters enumerated in List III in the Seventh Schedule (in this Constitution referred to as the "Concurrent List").

(3) Subject to clauses (1) and (2), the Legislature of any State has exclusive power to make laws for such State or any part thereof with respect to any of the matters enumerated in List II in the Seventh Schedule (in this Constitution referred to as the "State List").

(4) Parliament has power to make laws with respect to any matter for any part of the territory of India not included in a State notwithstanding that such matter is a matter enumerated in the State List.

Relevant entries in List I—Union List

82 Taxes on income other than agricultural income.

83 Duties of customs including export duties.

84 Duties of excise on tobacco and other goods manufactured or produced in India except—

(*a*) alcoholic liquors for human consumption;

(*b*) opium, Indian hemp and other narcotic drugs and narcotics,

but including medicinal and toilet preparations containing

alcohol or any substance included in sub-paragraph (b) of this entry.

85 Corporation tax.

86 Taxes on the capital value of the assets, exclusive of agricultural land, of individuals and companies; taxes on the capital of companies.

87 Estate duty in respect of property other than agricultural land.

88 Duties in respect of succession to property other than agricultural land.

89 Terminal taxes on goods and passengers, carried by railway, sea or air; taxes on railway fares and freights.

90 Taxes other than stamp duties on transactions in stock exchanges and future markets.

91 Rates of stamp duty in respect of bills of exchange, cheques, promissory notes, bills of lading, letters of credit, policies of insurance, transfer of shares, debentures, proxies and receipts.

92 Taxes on the sale or purchase of newspapers and on advertisements published therein.

92A Taxes on the sale or purchase of goods other than newspapers, where such sale or purchase takes place in the course of inter-State trade or commerce.

Relevant entries in List II—State List

45 Land revenue, including the assessment of collection of revenue, the maintenance of land records, survey for revenue purposes and records of rights, and alienation of revenues.

46 Taxes on agricultural income.

47 Duties in respect of succession to agricultural land.

48 Estate duty in respect of agricultural land.

49 Taxes on lands and building.

50 Taxes on mineral rights subject to any limitations imposed by Parliament by law relating to mineral development.

51 Duties of excise on the following goods manufactured or produced in the State and countervailing duties at the

same or lower rates on similar goods manufactured or produced elsewhere in India—

(*a*) alcoholic liquors for human consumption;

(*b*) opium, Indian hemp and other narcotic drugs and narcotics;

but not including medicinal and toilet preparations containing alcohol or any substance included in sub-paragraph (b) of this entry.

52 Taxes on the entry of goods into a local area for consumption, use or sale therein.

53 Taxes on the consumption or sale of electricity.

54 Taxes on the sale or purchase of goods other than newspapers, subject to the provisions of entry 92A of List I.

55 Taxes on advertisement other than advertisements published in the newspapers and advertisements broadcast by radio or television.

56 Taxes on goods and passengers carried by road or on inland waterways.

57 Taxes on vehicles, whether mechanically propelled or not, suitable for use on roads, including tramcars subject to the provisions of entry 35 of List III.

58 Taxes on animals and boats.

59 Tolls.

60 Taxes on professions, trades, callings and employments.

61 Capitation taxes.

62 Taxes on luxuries, including taxes on entertainments, amusements, betting and gambling.

63 Rates of stamp duty in respect of documents other than those specified in the provisions of List I with regard to rates of stamp duty.

Article 268. Duties levied by the Union but collected and appropriated by the States.

(1) Such stamp duties and such duties of excise on medicinal and toilet preparations as are mentioned in the Union List shall be levied by the Government of India but shall be collected—

(*a*) in the case where such duties are leviable within any Union Territory, by the Government of India, and

(*b*) in other cases, by the States within which such duties are respectively leviable.

(2) The proceeds in any financial year of any such duty leviable within any State shall not form part of the Consolidated Fund of India, but shall be assigned to that State.

Article 269. Taxes levied and collected by the Union but assigned to the States.

(1) The following duties and taxes shall be levied and collected by the Government of India but shall be assigned to the States in the manner provided in clause (2), namely—

(*a*) duties in respect of succession to property other than agricultural land;

(*b*) estate duty in respect of property other than agricultural land;

(*c*) terminal taxes on goods or passengers carried by railway, sea or air;

(*d*) taxes on railway fares and freights;

(*e*) taxes other than stamp duties on transactions in stock exchanges and future markets;

(*f*) taxes on the sale or purchase of newspapers and on advertisements published therein;

(*g*) taxes on the sale or purchase of goods other than newspapers, where such sale or purchase takes place in the course of inter-State trade or commerce.

(2) The net proceeds in any financial year of any such duty or tax, except in so far as those proceeds represent proceeds attributable to Union territories, shall not form part of the Consolidated Fund of India, but shall be assigned to the States within which that duty or tax is leviable in that year, and shall be distributed among those States in accordance with such principles of distribution as may be formulated by Parliament by law.

(3) Parliament may by law formulate principles for determining when a sale or purchase of goods takes place in the course of inter-State trade or commerce.

Article 270. Taxes levied and collected by the Union and distributed between the Union and the States.

(1) Taxes on income other than agricultural income shall be levied and collected by the Government of India and distributed between the Union and the States in the manner provided in clause (2).

(2) Such percentage, as may be prescribed, of the net proceeds in any financial year of any such tax, except in so far as those proceeds represent proceeds attributable to Union territories or to taxes payable in respect of Union emoluments, shall not form part of the Consolidated Fund of India, but shall be assigned to the States within which that tax is leviable in that year, and shall be distributed among those States in such manner and from such time as may be prescribed.

(3) For the purpose of clause (2), in each financial year such percentage as may be prescribed of so much of the net proceeds of taxes on income as does not represent the net proceeds of taxes payable in respect of Union emoluments shall be deemed to represent proceeds attributable to Union territories.

(4) In this article—

(*a*) "taxes on income" does not include a corporation tax;

(*b*) "prescribed" means—

(*i*) until a Finance Commission has been constituted, prescribed by the President by order, and

(*ii*) after a Finance Commission has been constituted, prescribed by the President by order after considering the recommendations of the Finance Commission;

(*c*) "Union emoluments" includes all emoluments and pensions payable out of the Consolidated Fund of India in respect of which income-tax is chargeable.

Article 271. Surcharge on certain duties and taxes for purposes of the Union.

Notwithstanding anything in Articles 269 and 270, Parliament may at any time increase any of the duties or taxes referred to in those articles by a surcharge for purposes of the Union and the whole proceeds of any such surcharge shall form part of the Consolidated Fund of India.

Article 272. Taxes which are levied and collected by the Union and may be distributed between the Union and the States.

Union duties of excise other than such duties of excise on medicinal and toilet preparations as are mentioned in the Union List shall be levied and collected by the Government of India, but, if Parliament by law so provides, there shall be paid out of the Consolidated Fund of India to the States to which the law imposing the duty extends sums equivalent to the whole or any part of the net proceeds of that duty, and those sums shall be distributed among those States in accordance with such principles of distribution as may be formulated by such laws.

Article 274. Prior recommendation of President required to Bills affecting taxation in which States are interested.

(1) No Bill or amendment which imposes or varies any tax or duty in which States are interested, or which varies the meaning of the expression "agricultural income" as defined for the purposes of the enactments relating to Indian income-tax, or which affects the principles on which under any of the foregoing provisions of this Chapter moneys are or may be distributable to States, or which impose any such surcharge for the purposes of the Union as is mentiond in the foregoing provisions of this Chapter, shall be introduced or moved in either House of Parliament except on the recommendations of the President.

(2) In this article, the expression "tax or duty in which States are interested" means—

(*a*) a tax or duty the whole or part of the net proceeds whereof are assigned to any States; or

(*b*) a tax or duty by reference to the net proceeds whereof sums are for the time being payable out of the Consolidated Fund of India to any State.

Article 275. Grants from the Union to certain States.

(1) Such sums as Parliament may by law provide shall be charged on the Consolidated Fund of India in each year as grants-in-aid of the revenues of such States as Parliament may determine to be in need of assistance, and different sums may be fixed for different States:

Provided that there shall be paid out of the Consolidated Fund of India as grants-in-aid of the revenues of a State such capital and recurring sums as may be necessary to enable that State to meet the cost pf such schemes of development as may be undertaken by the State with the approval of the Government of India for the purpose of promoting the welfare of the Scheduled Tribes in that State or raising the level of the administration of the Scheduled Areas therein to that of the administration of the rest of the areas of that State:

Provided further that there shall be paid out of the Consolidated Fund of India as grants-in-aid of the revenues of the State of Assam sums capital and recurring equivalent to—

(*a*) the average excess of expenditure over the revenue during the two years immediately preceding the commencement of the Constitution in respect of the administration of the tribal areas specified in Part A of the table appended to paragraph 20 of the Sixth Schedule; and

(*b*) the cost of such schemes of development as may be undertaken by that State with the approval of the Government of India for the purpose of raising the level of administration of the said areas to that of the administration of the rest of the areas of that State.

(2) Until provision is made by Parliament under clause (1), the powers conferred on Parliament under that clause shall be exercisable by the President by order and any order made by the President under this clause shall have effect subject to any provision so made by Parliament:

Provided that after a Finance Commission has been constituted no order shall be made under this clause by the

President except after considering therecom mendations of the Finance Commission.

Article 279. Calculation of "net proceeds", etc.

(1) In the foregoing provisions of this Chapter, "net proceeds" means in relation to any tax or duty the proceeds thereof reduced by the cost of collection, and for the purposes of those provisions the net proceeds of any tax or duty, or of any part of any tax or duty, in or attributable to any area shall be ascertained and certified by the Comptroller and Auditor-General of India, whose certificate shall be final.

(2) Subject as aforesaid, and to any other express provision of this Chapter, a law made by Parliament or an order of the President may, in any case where under this part the proceeds of any duty or tax are, or may be, assigned to any State, provide for the manner in which the proceeds are to be calculated, for the time from or at which and the manner in which any payments are to be made, for the making of adjustments between one financial year and another, and for any other incidental or ancillary matters.

Article 280. Finance Commission.

(1) The President shall, within two years from the commencement of this Commission and thereafter at the expiration of every fifth year or at such earlier time as the President considers necessary, by order constitute a Finance Commission which shall consist of a Chairman and four other members to be appointed by the President.

(2) Parliament may by law determine the qualifications which shall be requisite for appointment as members of the Commission and the manner in which they shall be selected.

(3) It shall be the duty of the Commission to make recommendations to the President as to—

(*a*) the distribution between the Union and the States, of the net proceeds of taxes which are to be, or may be, divided between them under this Chapter and the allocation between the States of the respective shares of such proceeds;

(*b*) the principles which should govern the grants-in-aid of the revenues of the States out of the Consolidated Fund of India;

(*c*) any other matter referred to the Commission by the President in the interests of sound finance.

(4) The Commission shall determine their procedure and shall have such powers in the performance of their functions as Parliament may by law confer on them.

Article 281. Recommendations of the Finance Commission.

The President shall cause every recommendation made by the Finance Commission under the provisions of this Constitution together with an explanatory memorandum as to the action taken thereon to be laid before each House of Parliament.

Article 282. Expenditure defrayable by the Union or a State out of its revenues.

The Union or a State may make any grants for any public purpose, notwithstanding that the purpose is not one with respect to which Parliament or the Legislature of the State, as the case may be, may make laws.

APPENDIX II

SUMMARY OF THE MAIN RECOMMENDATIONS OF THE EIGHTH FINANCE COMMISSION

A. Shares of Central Taxes and Duties

I. *Income tax*

(1) Out of the net proceeds, a sum equal to 1.792 per cent thereof shall be deemed to represent the proceeds attributable to Union territories;

(2) The share of net income tax proceeds, except the portion representing the proceeds attributable to Union territories and Union emoluments, to be assigned to the States should be 85 per cent ; and

(3) The distribution amongst the States *inter se* of the share assigned to the States in respect of each financial year should be on the basis of the percentages shown in the table below :

State	Percentage with Sikkim (If the income tax becomes leviable in that State)	State	Percentage with Sikkim (If the income tax becomes leviable in that State)
1. Andhra Pradesh	8.18	13. Meghalaya	0.18
2. Assam	2.78	14. Nagaland	0.09
3. Bihar	12.08	15. Orissa	4.20
4. Gujarat	4.41	16. Punjab	1.74
5. Haryana	1.07	17. Rajasthan	4.54
6. Himachal Pradesh	0.55	18. Sikkim	0 03
7. Jammu & Kashmir	0.84	19. Tamil Nadu	7.56
8. Karnataka	4.97	20. Tripura	0.27
9. Kerala	3.76	21. Uttar Pradesh	17.91
10. Madhya Pradesh	8.38	22. West Bengal	7.80
11. Maharashtra	8.39		
12. Manipur	0.22	Total :	100.00

II. *Union duties of excise*

(1) States should be paid a share out of the net proceeds of all excise duties, except the duties collected under the provisions of Additional Excise Duties (Textiles and Textile Articles) Act, 1978, and cesses earmarked by law for special purposes.

(2) The net proceeds of the entire excise duty on generation of electricity should be distributed among the States in an amount equal to the collections in or attributable to that State.

(3) The States' share in the net proceeds of shareable excise duties, excluding that on electricity, should be 45 per cent.

(4) Forty per cent of the net proceeds of shareable excise duties, excluding that on electricity, should be distributed among all the States on the basis of the percentages shown in the table below against their names.

State	Percentage	State	Percentage
1. Andhra Pradesh	8.59	12. Manipur	0.23
2. Assam	2.98	13. Meghalaya	0.19
3. Bihar	13.20	14. Nagaland	0.10
4. Gujarat	3.51	15. Orissa	4.59
5. Haryana	1.02	16. Punjab	1.32
6. Himachal Pradesh	0.59	17. Rajasthan	4.69
7. Jammu & Kashmir	0.86	18. Sikkim	0.04
8. Karnataka	5.08	19. Tamil Nadu	7.32
9. Kerala	3.80	20. Tripura	0.29
10. Madhya Pradesh	8.85	21. Uttar Pradesh	19.10
11. Maharashtra	6.22	22. West Bengal	7.45
		Total :	100.00

(5) The balance of 5 per cent of the net proceeds of shareable excise duties excluding that on electricity should be distributed among the deficit States in each of the five years commencing from 1.4.1984 on the basis of the percentages shown respectively in columns 2, 3, 4, 5 and 6 of the table below:

State	Share in 5 per cent to Deficit States (%)				
	1984-85	85-86	86-87	87-88	88-89
1. Assam	12.72*	12.58	12.71	13 42	12.02
2. Himachal Pradesh	10.34	11.53	12.91	14.10	16.47
3. Jammu & Kashmir	15.46	16.66	17.82	18.56	20.25
4. Manipur	6.97	7.74	8.72	9.55	11.22
5. Meghalaya	5.57	6.18	6.94	7.57	8.86
6. Nagaland	8.84	9.94	11.24	12 37	14.48
7. Orissa	9.21	8.15	5.46	3.11	0.60
8. Rajasthan	1.94	—	—	—	—
9. Sikkim	1.66	1.84	2.05	2.23	2.59
10. Tripura	8.20	9.10	10.21	11.16	12 96
11. West Bengal	19.08	16.27	11.93	7.94	0.54
Total :	100.00	100.00	100.00	100 00	100.00

*Figures have been rounded off and are correct up to two decimal places.

III. *Additional duties of excise in replacement of sales tax*

The net proceeds of the additional excise duties on textiles, sugar and tobacco should be distributed on the following basis:

(*a*) A sum equal to 2.391 per cent of such net proceeds be retained by the Central Government as attributable to the Union territories.

(*b*) The balance should be distributed amongst the States in accordance with the percentage mentioned below:

State	Percentage	State	Percentage
1. Andhra Pradesh	7.504	12. Manipur	0.178
2. Assam	2.566	13. Meghalaya	0.183
3. Bihar	8.627	14. Nagaland	0.098
4. Gujarat	5.941	15. Orissa	3.653
5. Haryana	2.488	16. Punjab	3.675
6. Himachal Pradesh	0.663	17. Rajasthan	4.827
7. Jammu & Kashmir	0.853	18. Sikkim	0.039
8. Karnataka	5.561	19. Tamil Nadu	7.549
9. Kerala	3.963	20. Tripura	0.287
10. Madhya Pradesh	6.942	21. Uttar Pradesh	14.318
11. Maharashtra	11.461	22. West Bengal	8.624
		Total :	100.000

IV. *Estate duty*

(1) The net proceeds of Estate Duty in respect of property other than agricultural land attributable to Union territories should be determined in the same manner and on the same principles as for the determination of the shares of each State, taking the Union territories as one unit for the purpose;

(2) The balance of the net proceeds of Estate Duty in each year should be distributed among the States, in proportion to the gross value of the immovable property and property other than immovable property taken together, located in each State and brought into assessment. The location of property other than immovable property should be determined in accordance with the rules framed under the Estate Duty Act, 1953. As for property located abroad, it should be deemed to be located in the State where it is brought to assessment; and

(3) Sikkim will also be entitled to a share in the net proceeds of this duty, calculated in the same manner as for the other States, as from the date the duty may become leviable in that State in the period covered by the Report.

V. *Grant-in-lieu of tax on railway passenger fares*

(1) The annual quantum of the grant in lieu of a tax on railway passenger fares be raised to Rs. 95 crores in each of the years 1984-85 to 1988-89.

(2) The grant to be made available be distributed among the States as under:

State	Percentage	State	Percentage
1. Andhra Pradesh	7.68	12. Manipur	0.02
2. Assam	2.03	13. Meghalaya	0.05
3. Bihar	9.51	14 Nagaland	0.16
4. Gujarat	6.67	15. Orissa	1.58
5. Haryana	1.84	16. Punjab	3.88
6. Himachal Pradesh	0.14	17. Rajasthan	4.87
7. Jammu & Kashmir	0.95	18. Sikkim	0.01
8. Karnataka	3.43	19. Tamil Nadu	6.61
9. Kerala	3.18	20. Tripura	0.04
10. Madhya Pradesh	5.85	21. Uttar Pradesh	17.85
11. Maharashtra	15.70	22. West Bengal	7.95
		Total :	100.00

VI. *Grant on account of wealth tax on agricultural property*

The share of each State in the grant on account of wealth tax on agricultural property should be an amount equivalent to the net collection in that State in that year.

B. Grants-in-Aid

(1) To cover the deficits on revenue account, the following States be paid the sums specified against each of them as grants-in-aid of their revenues in the respective years indicated in the table below under the substantive part of clause (1) of Article 275 of the Constitution.

(*Rs. in crores*)

State	Total 1984-89	84-85	85-86	86-87	87-88	88-89
1. Assam	274.93	78.88	66.92	55.08	47.37	26.38
2. Himachal Pradesh	223.04	57.65	53.91	47.35	40.76	23.37
3. Jammu & Kashmir	329.18	89.22	81.14	68.79	57.34	32.69
4. Manipur	146.95	38.14	35.51	31.25	26.87	15.18
5. Meghalaya	119.15	30.92	28.76	25.30	21.75	12.42
6. Nagaland	190.52	48.76	45.96	40.65	35.19	19.96
7. Orissa	207.60	67.55	54.94	37.78	27.42	19.91
8. Rajasthan	42.63	34.25	8.38	—	—	—
9. Sikkim	36.16	9.38	8.71	7.66	6.59	3.82
10. Tripura	187.05	47.83	44.71	39.57	34.41	20.53
11. West Bengal	443.61	142.11	113.31	82.59	63.00	42.60
Total :	2200.22	644.39	542.25	436.02	360.70	216.86

(2) To cover the requirements of upgradation and special problems, during the five years commencing from 1st April 1984, the following States be paid the amount specified against each of them as grants-in-aid of their revenues under the substantive part of clause (1) of Article 275 of the Constitution. The annual payments be regulated as indicated in para 12.74 of the Report.

Grants for upgradation and special problems 1984-85

(Rs. crores)

State	For upgradation	For special problems	Total
1. Andhra Pradesh	80.49	—	80.49
2. Assam	58.35	5.00	63.35
3. Bihar	130.27	—	130.27
4. Himachal Pradesh	15.76	0.50	16.26
5. Jammu & Kashmir	46.07	2.48	48.55
6. Kerala	16.81	—	16.81
7. Madhya Pradesh	147.69	10.00	157.69
8. Manipur	20.30	2.00	22.30
9. Meghalaya	18.20	1.00	19.20
10. Nagaland	10.81	—	10.81
11. Orissa	74.84	—	74.84
12. Punjab	—	20.00	20.00
13. Rajasthan	43.48	10.00	53.48
14. Sikkim	3.14	1.00	4.14
15. Tripura	13.79	0.80	14.59
16. Uttar Pradesh	108.18	—	108.18
17. West Bengal	126.37	—	126.37
Total :	914.55	52.78	967.33

(3) To meet the margin money requirements of States they shall be entitled to the sums specified against each of them as grants-in-aid of their revenues in each of the five years commencing from 1st April, 1984, under the substantive portion of clause (1) of Article 275 of the Constitution, provided that these amounts shall be released as indicated in para (1)(c) of item C below:

State	Annual Grants (Rs. crores)	State	Annual Grants (Rs. crores)
1. Andhra Pradesh	12.250	12. Manipur	0.125
2. Assam	3.625	13. Meghalaya	0.125
3. Bihar	16.875	14. Nagaland	0.125
4. Gujarat	14.375	15. Orissa	13.125
5. Haryana	2.250	16. Punjab	3 000
6. Himachal Pradesh	0.875	17. Rajasthan	8.375
7. Jammu & Kashmir	0.750	18. Sikkim	0.125
8. Karnataka	3.000	19. Tamil Nadu	4.375
9. Kerala	2.500	20. Tripura	0.375
10. Madhya Pradesh	2.375	21. Uttar Pradesh	16.250
11. Maharashtra	3.625	22. West Bengal	11.875
		Total :	120.375

(4) Grants-in-aid under Article 275 of the Constitution to cover net additional interest liability on account of fresh borrowings and lendings in the period 1984-89 may be paid to the deficit States in each of the four years commencing from 1st April, 1985, as indicated in paragraph 13.16 of the Report.* Grants-in-aid, if any, may also be paid to the deficit States during the years 1985-86 to 1988-89 to cover the additional burden on account of committed expenditure in respect of Plan schemes completed in 1984-85 as mentioned in paragraph 13.16 of the Report.

*Report of the Eighth Finance Commission, 1984. We have not given recommendations on other terms of reference.

APPENDIX III

TRANSFERS TO THE STATES ON THE BASIS OF THE RECOMMENDATIONS OF THE FINANCE COMMISSIONS DURING 1951-52—1983-84

	Share in Divisible Taxes and Duties					Statutory and other grants				Grand Total
	Income tax	Union duties of excise: Basic	Union duties of excise: Additional	Estate Duty	Total	Article 275 grants	In lieu of tax on Railway Fares	Other grants	Total	
1	2	3	4	5	6	7	8	9	10	11
1st Five-Year Plan										
1951-52	53	...	...	...	53	1	...	16	17	70
1952-53	57	17	...	...	74	5	...	14	19	93
1953-54	57	15	...	...	72	7	...	14	21	93
1954-55	56	15	...	...	71	7	...	15	22	93
1955-56	55	17	...	2	74	7	...	17	24	98
Total :	**278**	**64**	...	**2**	**344**	**27**	...	**76**	**103**	**447**
2nd Five-Year Plan										
1956-57	59	18	...	2	79*	8	...	12	20	99
1957-58	74	29	11	2	116*	36	5	7	48	164
1958-59	76	33	40	2	151*	36	11	10	57	208
1959-60	79	36	39	3	157*	36	13	13	62	219
1960-61	87	37	38	3	165*	37	14	12	63	228
Total :	**375**	**153**	**128**	**12**	**668**	**153**	**43**	**54**	**250**	**918**

1	2	3	4	5	6	7	8	9	10	11
3rd Five-Year Plan										
1961-62	94	41	40	4	179	40	12	4	56	235
1962-63	95	79	46	4	224	61	12	7	80	304
1963-64	119	92	44	4	259	62	13	7	82	341
1964-65	124	86	41	7	258	65	13	10	88	346
1965-66	123	100	46	7	276	64	13	11	88	364
Total :	**555**	**398**	**217**	**26**	**1196**	**292**	**63**	**39**	**394**	**1590**
Three Annual Plans										
1966-67	137	184	47	5	373	141	16	12	169	542
1967-68	175	203	32	7	417	141	16	8	165	582
1968-69	195	241	50	6	492	141	16	9	166	658
Total :	**507**	**628**	**129**	**18**	**1282**	**423**	**48**	**29**	**500**	**1782**
4th Five-Year Plan										
1969 70	293	266	56	7	622	153	16	10	179	801
1970-71	359	318	72	6	755	142	16	13	171	926
1971-72	462	369	106	7	944	141	16	11	168	1112
1972-73	462	432	135	8	1067	146	16	15	177	1244
1973-74	532	465	166	11	1174	131	16	17	164	1338
Total :	**2138**	**1850**	**535**	**39**	**4562**	**713**	**80**	**66**	**859**	**5421**

5th Five-Year Plan										
1974-75	512	524	178	10	1224	482	16	8	506	1730
1975-76	734	646	211	8	1599	503	16	...	519	2118
1976-77	652	774	254	10	1690	500	16	...	516	2206
1977-78	676	817	303	10	1806	583	16	1	600	2406
1978-79	700	944	301	11	1956	615	16	1	632	2588
Total :	**3274**	**3705**	**1247**	**49**	**8275**	**2683**	**80**	**10**	**2773**	**11048**
6th Five-Year Plan										
1979-80	862	2201	330	11	3404	256	17	1	274	3678
1980-81	1003	2378	396	12	3789	281	16	1	298	4087
1981-82	1019	2759	462	17	4257	292	16	1	309	4566
1982-83 (RE)	1132	2999	492	16	4639	399	1o	Neg.	415	5054
1983-84 (BE)	1175	3293	604	16	5088	399	16	Neg.	415	5503
Total :	**5191**	**13630**	**2284**	**72**	**21177**	**1627**	**81**	**3**	**1711**	**22888**

*Does not take into account State 'share' in tax on railway passenger fares. These transfers are shown under 'Other grants'.

Source : Report of Seventh Finance Commission for data up to the year 1976-77 and State Budgets/Finance Accounts for later years.

APPENDIX IV

DISTRIBUTION OF INCOME AND EXCISE TAXES TO STATES AS RECOMMENDED BY VARIOUS FINANCE COMMISSIONS

	Coverage	% to be distributed among States	Basis of Distribution among States	Remarks
1	2	3	4	5
(*a*) **Income Tax**				
First F.C. (1952)	Net proceeds of taxes on income other than agricultural income excluding proceeds attributable to Union Territories and taxes payable in respect of the Union emoluments	55	80% population 20% collection	
Second F.C. (1957)		60	90% population 10% collection	100% population goal
Third F.C. (1961)		66-2/3	80% population 20% collection	
Fourth F.C. (1965)		75	80% population 20% collection	
Fifth F.C. (1969)	Advance tax collections included	75	90% population 10% assessment	

Sixth F.C. (1973)	No change	80	90% population 10% assessment	
Seventh F.C. (1978)	No change	85	90% population 10% assessment	
Eighth F.C. (1984)	No change	85	10% assessment 90% on the basis of (a) 25% weight to population, (b) 25% weight to projected population divided by State's income, (c) 50% weightage to formula of revenue equalisation as worked out by the Commission.	
(*b*) Excise Duties				
First F.C. (1952)	Tobacco, matches and vegetable products	40	100% population basis	Select excises on commodities of common and widespread consumption yielding a sizeable sum were included in order to ensure sizeable revenue and reasonable stability.

1	2	3	4	5
Second F.C. (1957)	Articles added: sugar, coffee, tea, paper and vegetable non-essential oils	25	90% population; 10% for adjustments	
Third F.C. (1961)	All commodities on which excise duties levied in 1960-61 except (i) those where yield is below Rs. 50 lakhs a year and (ii) motor spirit (treated differently).		Population major basis, but some adjustment was made on the basis of relative financial weakness, disparity in development, percentage of Scheduled Castes, Tribes etc.	Wide coverage because of need for broader base and inter-relation with sales tax.
Fourth F.C. (1965)	All excluding regulatory duties, special excises and earmarked cesses.	20	80% population and 20% relative economic and social backwardness, as measured by seven indicators.	Extension of same logic as by Third Finance Commission.
Fifth F.C. (1969)	All excluding regulatory duties and earmarked cesses; special excises to be included from 1972-73 onwards.	20	80% population and 20% economic and social backwardness, two-thirds of which distributed only among States with per capita	

			income below average per capita income of all States.
Sixth F.C. (1973)	All excluding auxiliary duties of excise for 1974-75 and 1975-76. However, from 1976-77 onwards, all including auxiliary duties of excise but excluding cesses.	20	75% population 25% relative economic and social backwardness, the distribution of this portion should be in relation to the distance of a State's per capita income from that of the State with the highest per capita income multiplied by the population of the State concerned.
Seventh F.C. (1976)	Entire net proceeds of Union excise duty on generation of electricity to be paid to the States. Besides, 40% of the net proceeds on all other articles excluding cesses.	40	Percentage share of each State in the divisible pool determined by assigning 25% weight to each of the following four factors : (a)

1	2	3	4	5
			Population by 1971 census (b) Projected population as on 1.3.1976 / Per capita State Domestic Product (c) Percentage of poor in total State population (d) Formula of revenue equalisation as worked out by the Commission.	
Eighth F.C. (1984)	No change. 45% of all other articles.	45	Percentage share of each state in the divisible pool determined by assigning (a) 25% weight to population as per the census of 1971 (b) 25%weight to the ratio of population to per capita State Domestic Product (c) 50% weight to the distance of the average per capita	

income of any state during 1976-79 from the state with highest per capita income (in this case Punjab).

Source : Government of India, *Report of the Finance Commission*, 1952, 1957, 1961, 1965, 1969, 1973 and 1978.

Highlights

1. As can be seen from the data presented above, each successive Finance Commission has recommended greater and greater transfer of resources of funds from the Centre to the States. This is reflected in the data on such transfers presented on the next page. The Seventh Finance Commission has taken one big step in the same direction.

2. The total transfers to all States, recommended by the Seventh Finance Commission, as shares of taxes and grants-in-aid are 55% of total divisible tax receipts and 26% of the total revenue receipts of the Central Government.

APPENDIX V

NOTE OF DISSENT BY PROF. RAJ KRISHNA TOTAL STATE ALLOCATIONS—MAJORITY REPORT AND THIS NOTE (1978-83)

	Majority (Rs. Crores)	Raj Krishna (Rs. Crores)
1. Andhra Pradesh	1522	1416
2. Assam	518	556
3. Bihar	2212	3143
4. Gujarat	963	758
5. Haryana	308	208
6. Himachal Pradesh	325	351
7. Jammu & Kashmir	376	404
8. Karnataka	1005	904
9. Kerala	770	843
10. Madhya Pradesh	1597	1837
11. Maharashtra	1714	1289
12. Manipur	194	194
13. Meghalaya	134	139
14. Nagaland	240	241
15. Orissa	984	1171
16. Punjab	419	249
17. Rajasthan	902	920
18. Sikkim	36	38
19. Tamil Nadu	1503	1613
20. Tripura	199	211
21. Uttar Pradesh	3314	3691
22. West Bengal	1597	1674

Source : Government of India, *Report of the Finance Commission, 1978.*

BIBLIOGRAPHY

Adarkar, B.P., *Principles and Problems of Federal Finance*, London: P.S. King, 1933.

Advisory Commission on Intergovernmental Relations, S 2948, 91st Congress, 1st Session, 1969.

Akerlof, C.A., Center-state fiscal relations in India, *Indian Economic Review*, Vol. IV, Oct. 1969.

Bhargava, R.N., (*The*) *Theory and Working of Union Finance in India*, London: Allen and Unwin, 1956.

Buchanan, J.M., Federalism and fiscal equity, *American Economic Review*, Vol. XL, September 1950.

Buchanan, J.M., Federal grants and resource allocation, *Journal of Political Economy*, No. 3, Vol. LX, 1952.

Chopra, O.P., An alternative approach for allocation of divisible resources, *Conference Number, Indian Ecomomic Association*, 1972.

Chopra, O.P., A probable criterion for evaluating justness of actual transfers - A case study of Indian states, *Indian Economic Review*, Vol. IX (New Series) No. 1, April 1974.

Chanda, Asok, *Federalism in India—a case study of Union-State Relations*, London: Allen and Unwin, 1965.

Ganguli, B.N., Federal state financial relations in U.S.A., Canada and Australia and their lessons for India in *Changing India*—Essays in honour of D.K. Gadgil, 1961.

Government of India, *Report of the Finance Commission*, 1951.

Government of India, *Report of the Finance Commission*, 1956.

Government of India, *Report of the Finance Commission*, 1961.

Government of India, *Report of the Finance Commission*, 1965.

Government of India, *Report of the Finance Commission*, 1969.

Government of India, *Report of the Finance Commission*, 1973.

Government of India, *Report of the Finance Commission*, 1978.

Government of India, *Report of the Finance Commission*, 1984.

Government of India, *Report of the Study Team on the Centre-State Relationships*, June 1969.

Government of India, Administrative Reforms Commission, *Report on the Centre-State Relations*, June 1969.

Haskell, N.A., Federal grants-in-aid, their influence on the state and local expenditure, *National Tax Journal*, Vol. XIX, 1966.

Hicks, J.R., The nature and basis of economic growth, in *Federalism and Economic Growth in Underdeveloped Areas* edited, U.K. Hicks, London: Allen and Unwin, 1961.

Hicks, U.K., Current problems of federal finances in India and some comparisons with Australia, *Public Finance*, No. 3, Vol. XXIII, 1968.

Hopkins, Thomas D., Income distribution in grants-in-aid equity analysis, *National Tax Journal*, Vol. XVIII, 1965.

Johnson, Darwin G., and Charles M. Mohan, Revenue sharing and the supply of public goods, *National Tax Journal*, June 1971.

Lakdawala, D.T., Some problems of Indian federal finance, *Commerce* (Annual) Vol. III, No. 2852, December 1965.

Lakdawala, D.T., *Union-State Financial Relations*, Bombay: Lalvani Publishing House, 1967.

Musgrave, R.A., Approaches to fiscal theory of political federalism, in National Bureau of Economic Research, *Public Finances: Needs, Sources and Utilisation*, edited James Buchanan, Princeton University Press, 1961.

Nixon Administration Proposal, S. 2948, 1st Congress, 1st Session, 1969.

Royal Commission on Taxation, Report, Ottawa, Queen's Printers, 1967.

Santhanam, K., Financial relations between the union and the states, *Commerce*, (Annual), Vol. 3, No. 2852, December 1965.

Sastri, K.V.S., *Federal State Fiscal Relations in India*, London: Oxford University Press, 1966.

Scott, A.D., A note on grants in federal countries, *Economica*, New Series, Vol. XVII, Nov. 1950.

Scott, A.D., Federal grants and resource allocation, *Journal of Political Economy*, No. 6, Vol. LX, 1952.

Scott, A.D., Evaluation of federal grants, *Economica*, New Series, Vol. XIX, Nov. 1952.

Scott, A.D., Economic goals of federal finance, *Public Finance*, No. 3, Vol. XIX, 1964.

Throw, Lester, The theory of grants-in-aid, *National Tax Journal*, Vol. XIX, December, 1966.

Tiebout, C.M., An economic theory of fiscal decentralisation, in National Bureau of Economic Research, *Public Finances: Needs, Sources and Utilisation*, edited James Buchanan, Princeton University Press, 1961.

Tripathi, R.N., *Federal Finance in a Developing Economy*, Calcutta: World Press, 1961.

Weidenbaum, Murray L., and Robert L. Joss, Alternative approaches to revenue sharing: A description and framework for evaluation, *National Tax Journal*, March 1970.

Zaveri, N.J., Transfer of non-plan resources to States, *Economic and Political Weekly*, Vol. 4, No. 23, June 7, 1966.

INDEX